BEN 10 RETURNS

ADAPTED BY Elizabeth Hurchalla
ADAPTATION DESIGNED AND LETTERED BY
Tomás Montalvo-Lagos

Ballantine Books * New York

A Del Rey Trade Paperback Original

CARTOON NETWORK, the logo, BEN 10 ALIEN FORCE, and all related characters and elements are trademarks of and © 2008 Cartoon Network. Used under license by Random House, Inc.

Published in the United States by Del Rey, an imprint of The Random House Publishing Group, a division of Random House, Inc., New York.

DEL REY is a registered trademark and the Del Rey colophon is a trademark of Random House, Inc.

ISBN 978-0-345-51438-7

Printed in the United States of America

www.delreymanga.com

9 8 7 6 5 4 3 2 1

Adaptation editor: Elizabeth Hurchalla
Graphic designer and letterer: Tomás Montalvo-Lagos

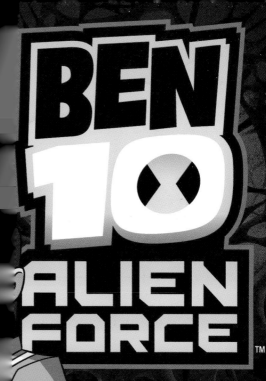

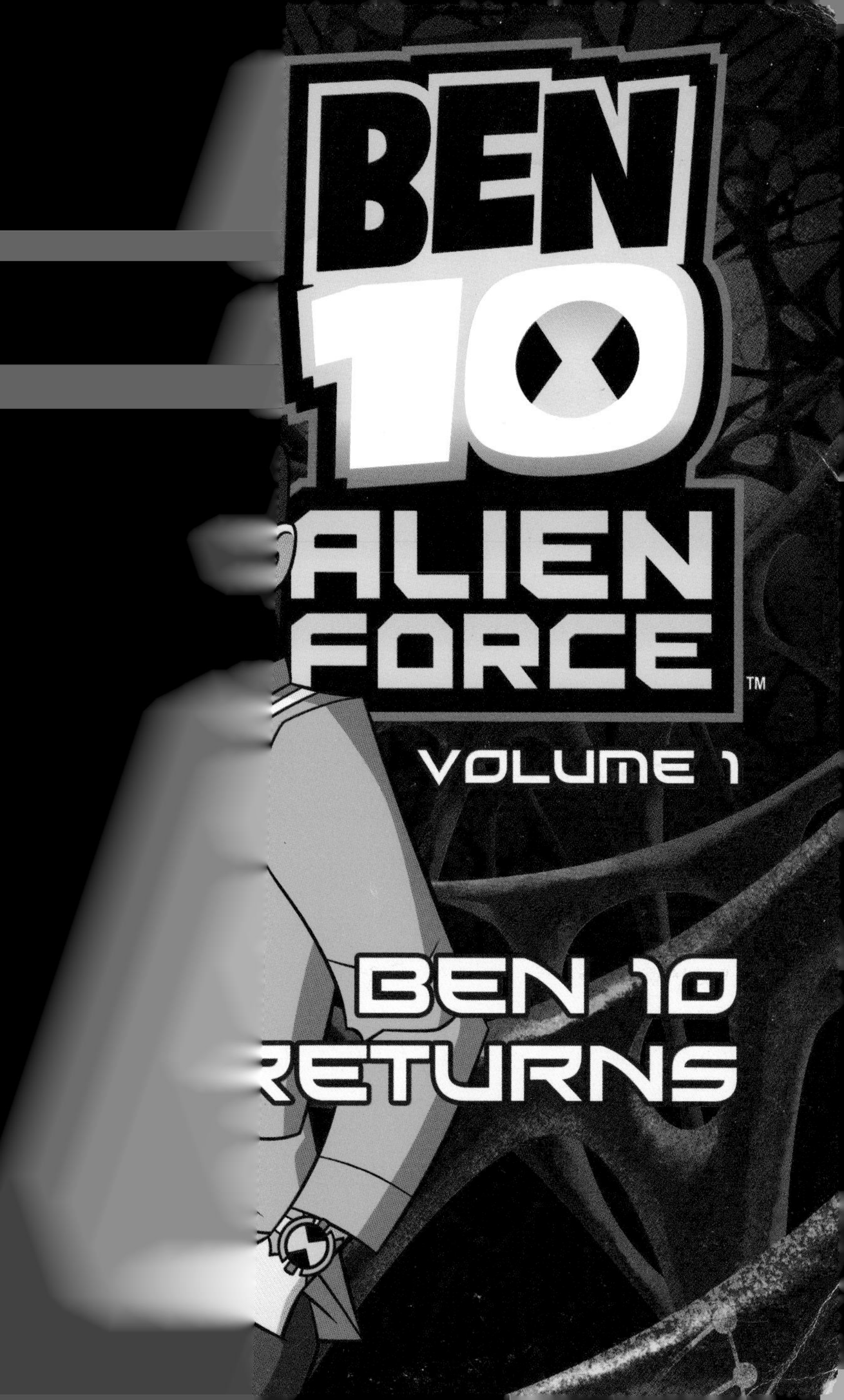

BEN 10
ALIEN FORCE™

VOLUME 1

BEN 10 RETURNS

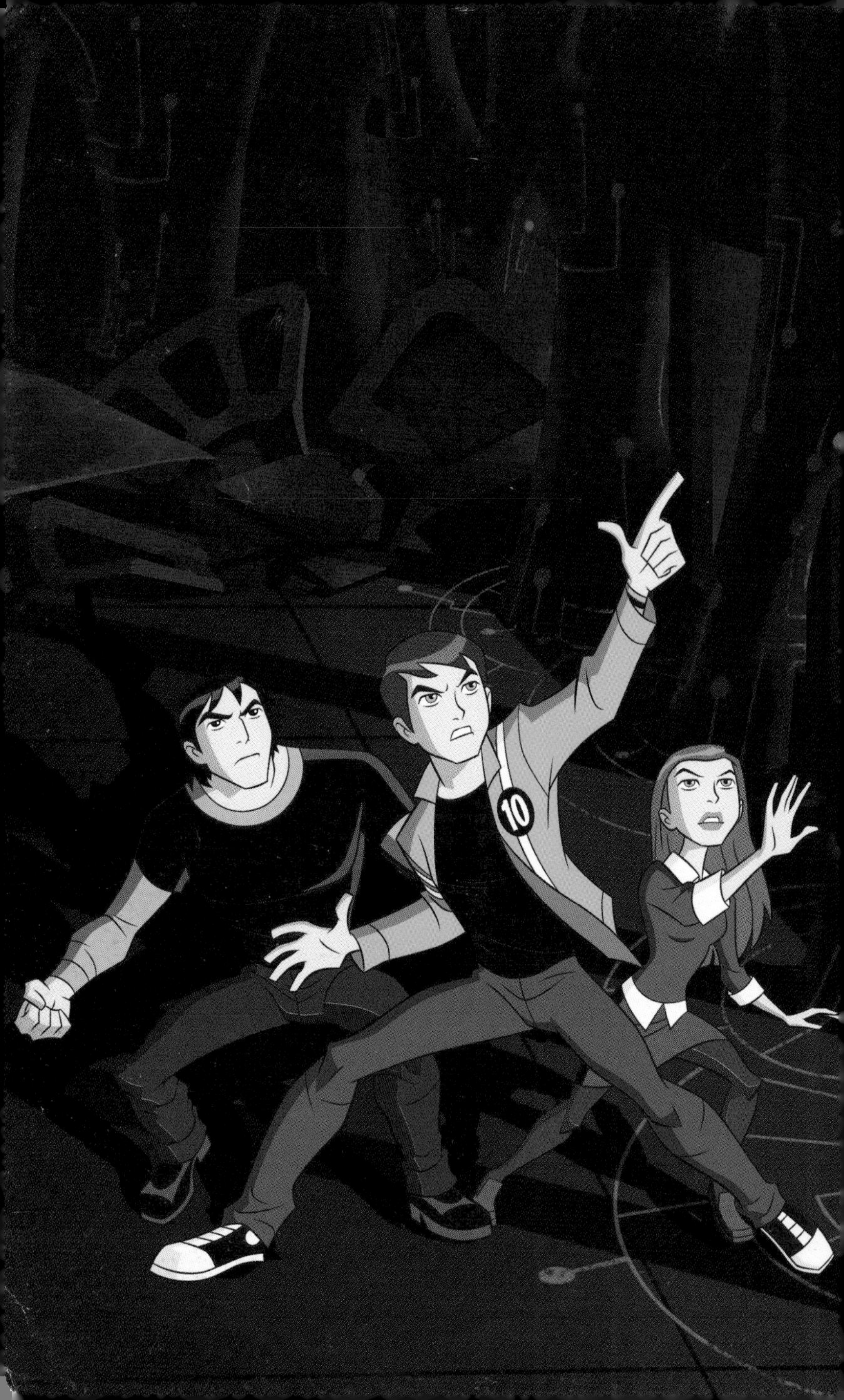
10

TABLE of CONTENTS

CAST OF BEN 10 ALIEN FORCE™

BEN TENNYSON

NOW 15, BEN IS AS ADVENTUROUS AS EVER. BUT WITH GRANDPA MAX MISSING, HE MUST ALSO BECOME A RESPONSIBLE LEADER. THE OMNITRIX HAS RECALIBRATED, ALLOWING BEN TO ACCESS A NEW SET OF ALIEN HEROES.

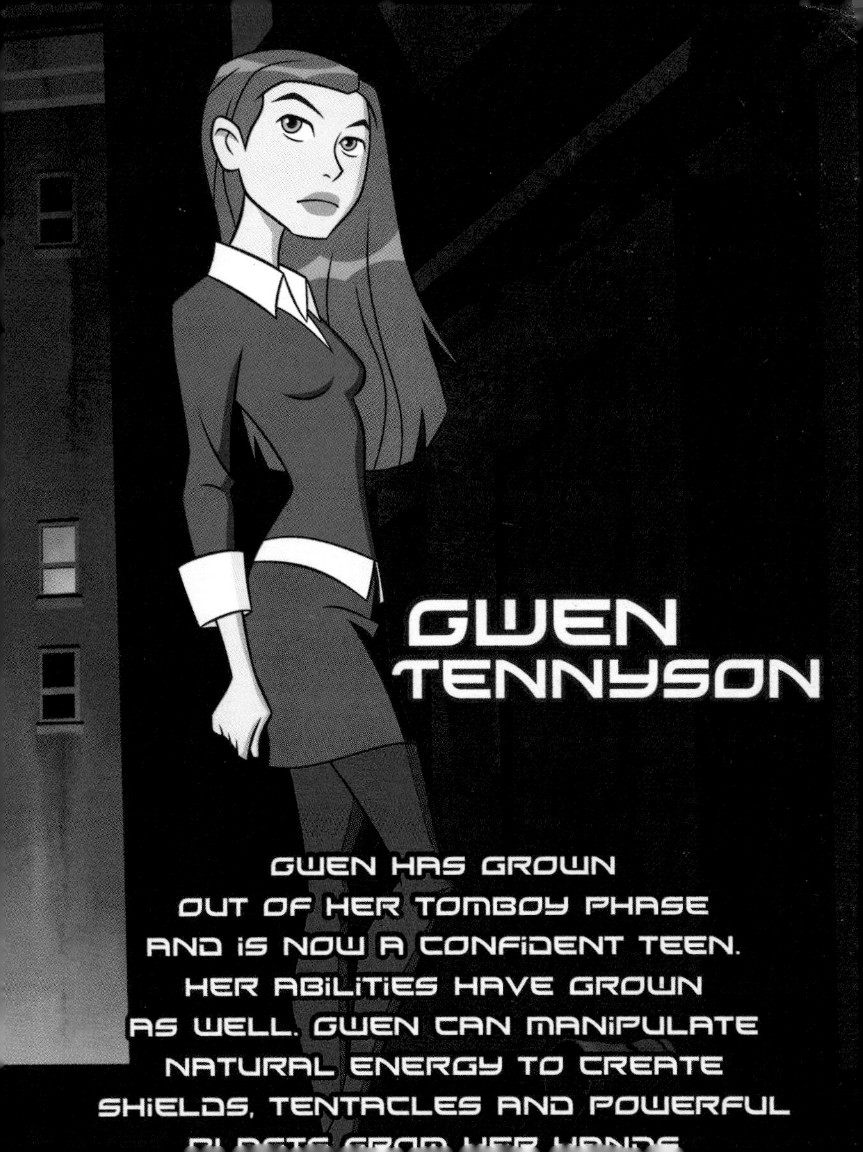

GWEN TENNYSON

GWEN HAS GROWN OUT OF HER TOMBOY PHASE AND IS NOW A CONFIDENT TEEN. HER ABILITIES HAVE GROWN AS WELL. GWEN CAN MANIPULATE NATURAL ENERGY TO CREATE SHIELDS, TENTACLES AND POWERFUL BLASTS FROM HER HANDS.

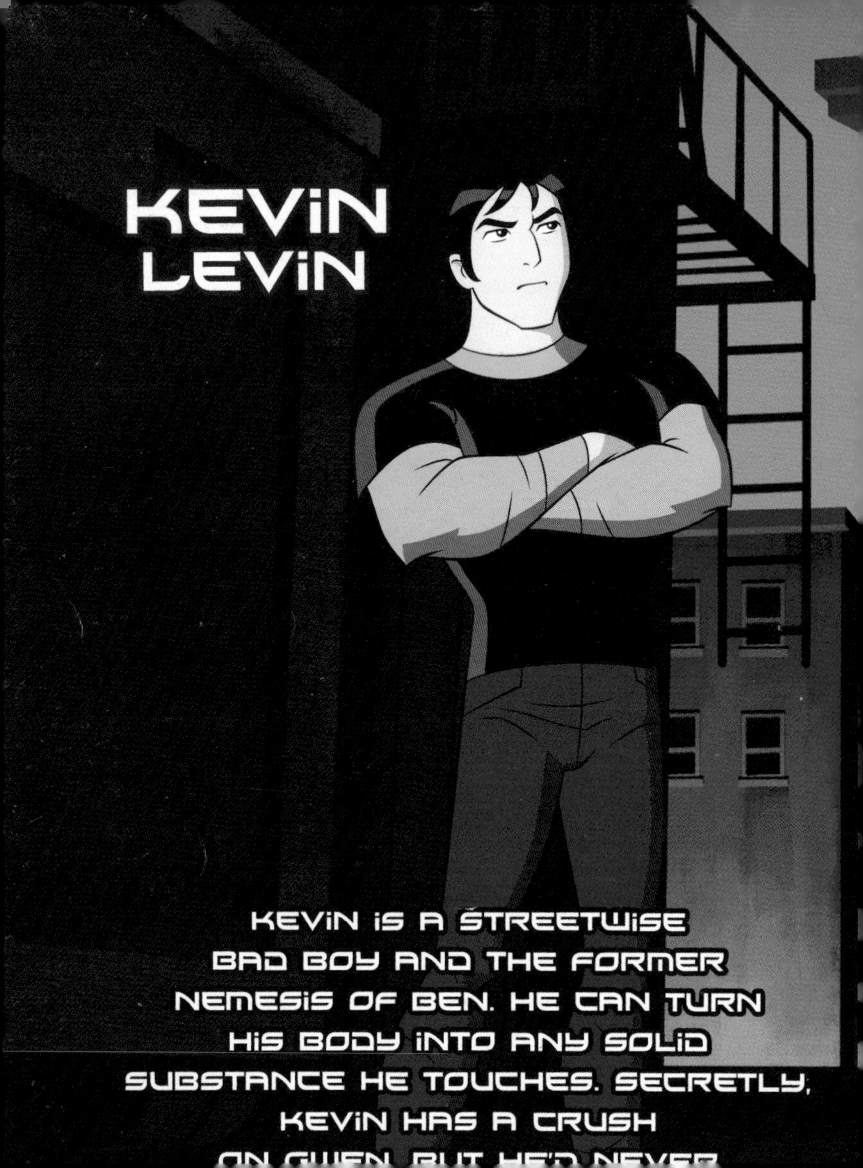

KEVIN LEVIN

KEVIN IS A STREETWISE BAD BOY AND THE FORMER NEMESIS OF BEN. HE CAN TURN HIS BODY INTO ANY SOLID SUBSTANCE HE TOUCHES. SECRETLY, KEVIN HAS A CRUSH ON GWEN, BUT HE'D NEVER

MAX TENNYSON

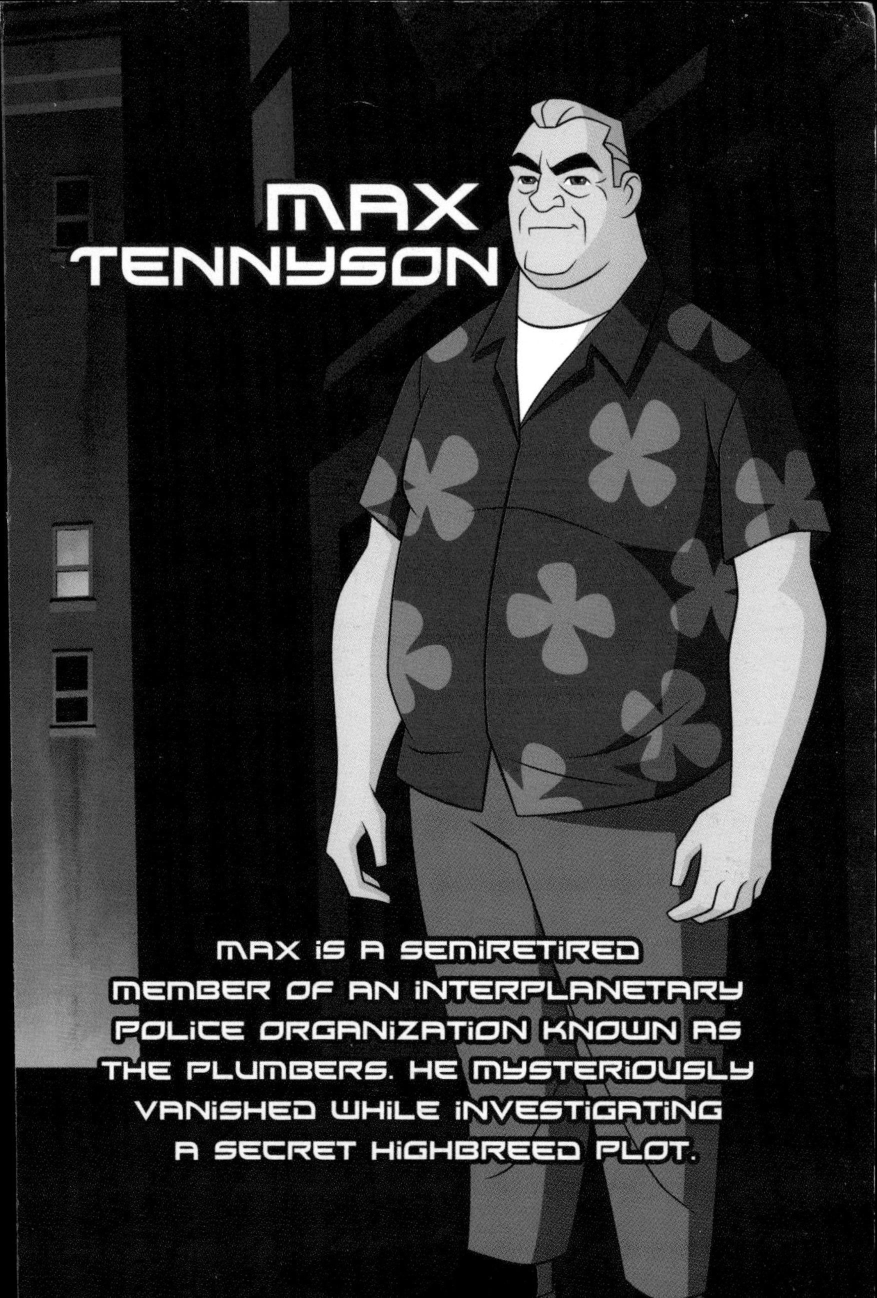

MAX IS A SEMIRETIRED MEMBER OF AN INTERPLANETARY POLICE ORGANIZATION KNOWN AS THE PLUMBERS. HE MYSTERIOUSLY VANISHED WHILE INVESTIGATING A SECRET HIGHBREED PLOT.

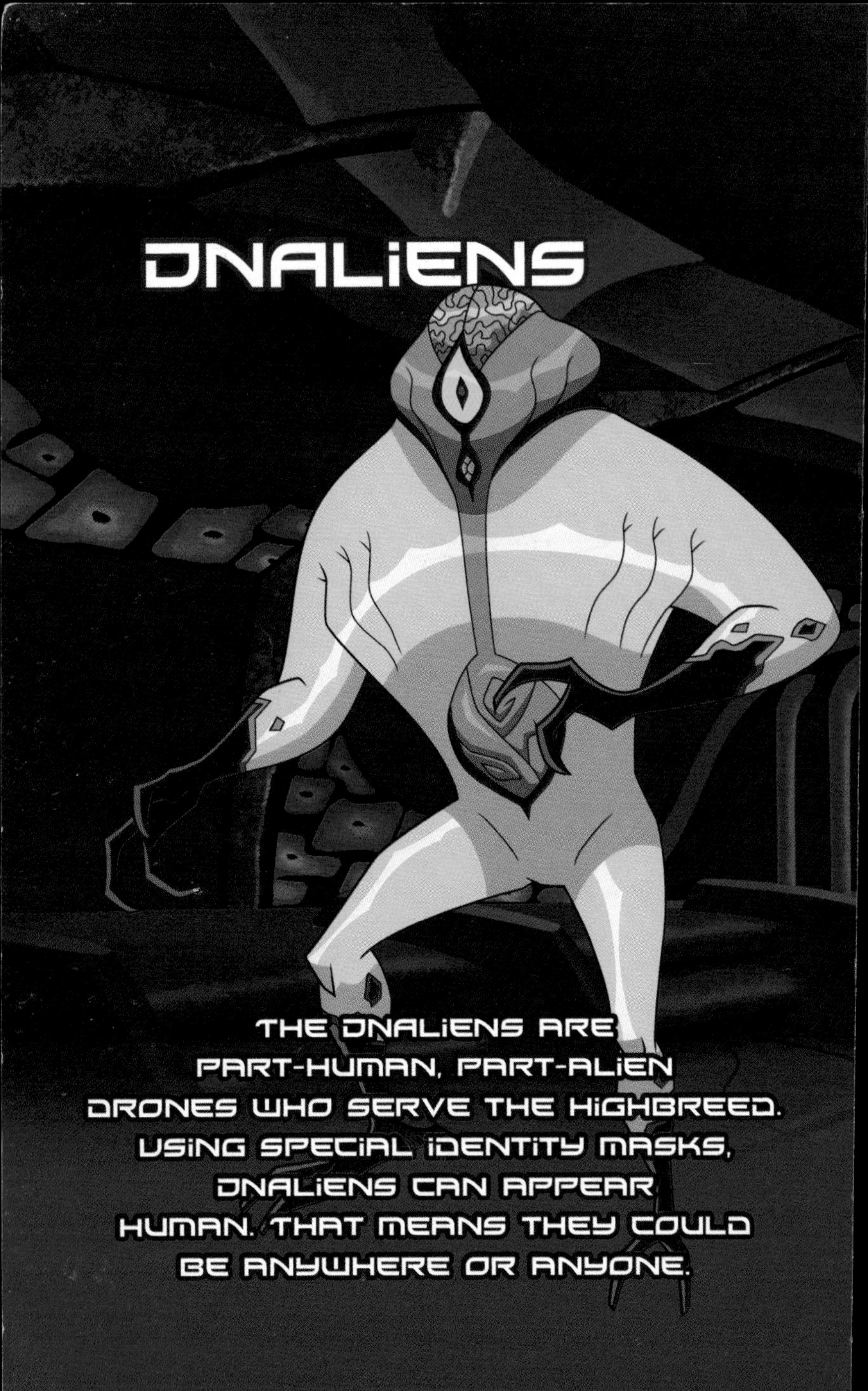

DNALIENS

THE DNALIENS ARE PART-HUMAN, PART-ALIEN DRONES WHO SERVE THE HIGHBREED. USING SPECIAL IDENTITY MASKS, DNALIENS CAN APPEAR HUMAN. THAT MEANS THEY COULD BE ANYWHERE OR ANYONE.

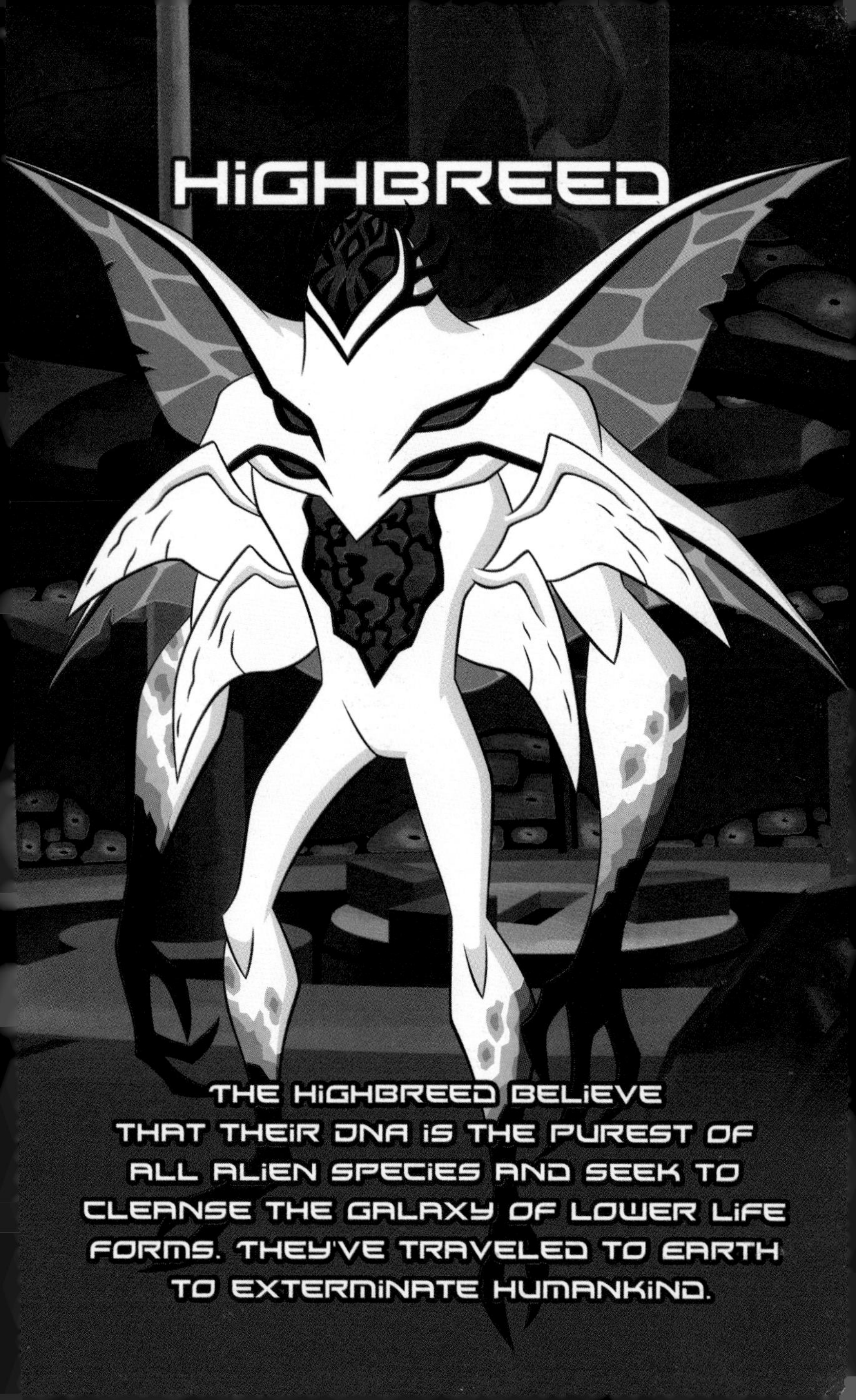

HIGHBREED

THE HIGHBREED BELIEVE THAT THEIR DNA IS THE PUREST OF ALL ALIEN SPECIES AND SEEK TO CLEANSE THE GALAXY OF LOWER LIFE FORMS. THEY'VE TRAVELED TO EARTH TO EXTERMINATE HUMANKIND.

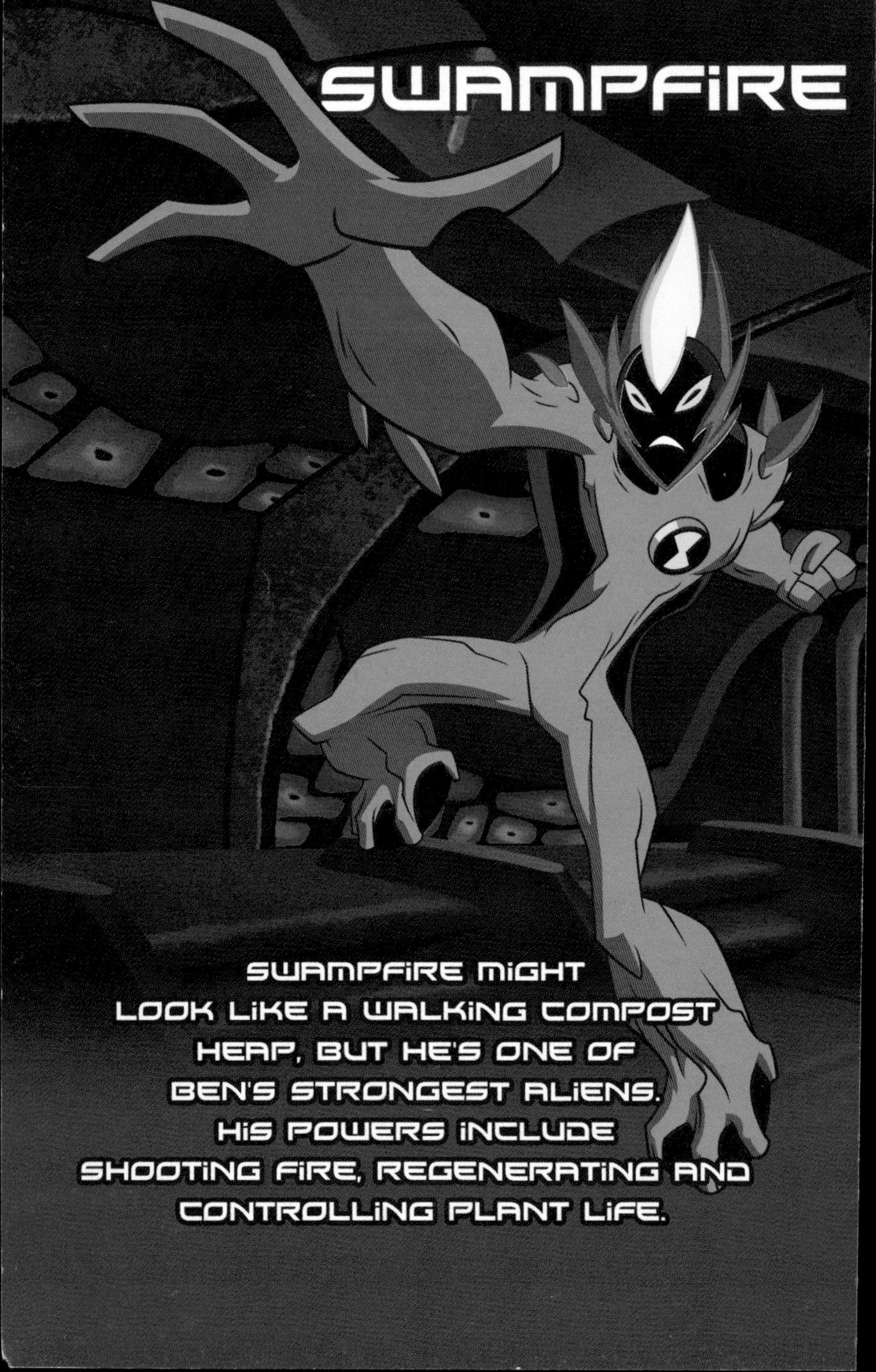

SWAMPFIRE

SWAMPFIRE MIGHT LOOK LIKE A WALKING COMPOST HEAP, BUT HE'S ONE OF BEN'S STRONGEST ALIENS. HIS POWERS INCLUDE SHOOTING FIRE, REGENERATING AND CONTROLLING PLANT LIFE.

FOREVER KNIGHTS

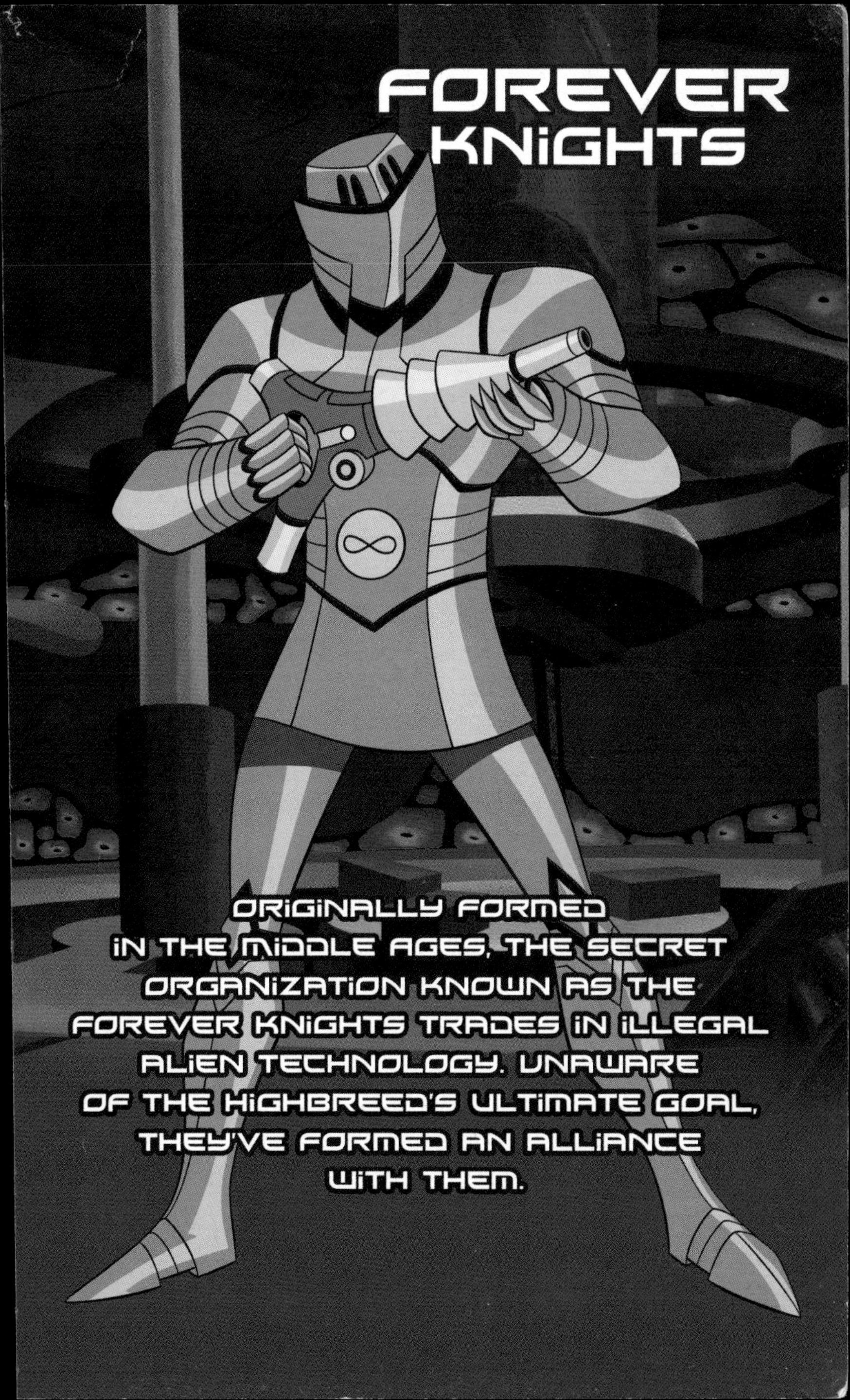

ORIGINALLY FORMED IN THE MIDDLE AGES, THE SECRET ORGANIZATION KNOWN AS THE FOREVER KNIGHTS TRADES IN ILLEGAL ALIEN TECHNOLOGY. UNAWARE OF THE HIGHBREED'S ULTIMATE GOAL, THEY'VE FORMED AN ALLIANCE WITH THEM.

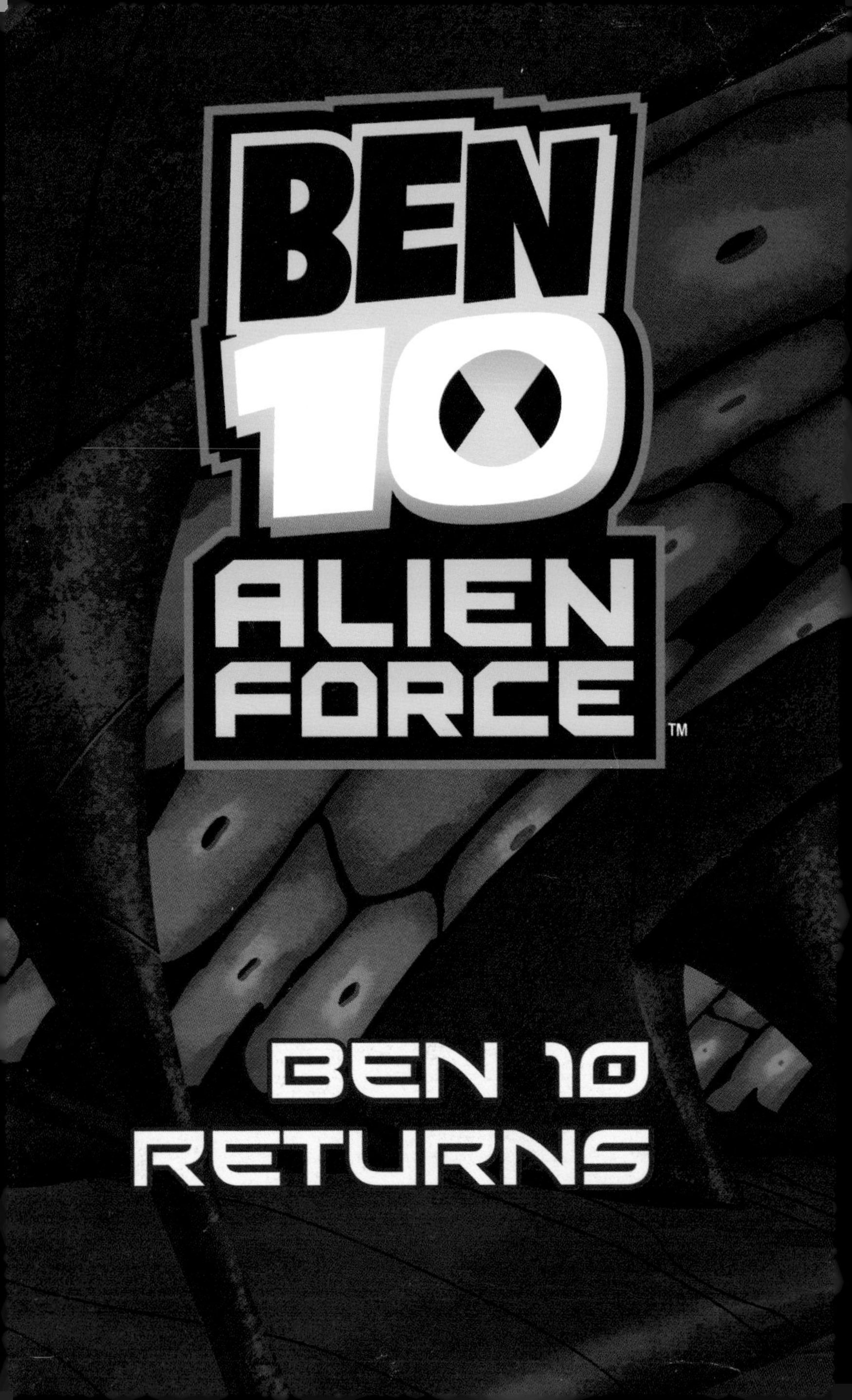

BEN 10 ALIEN FORCE™

BEN 10 RETURNS

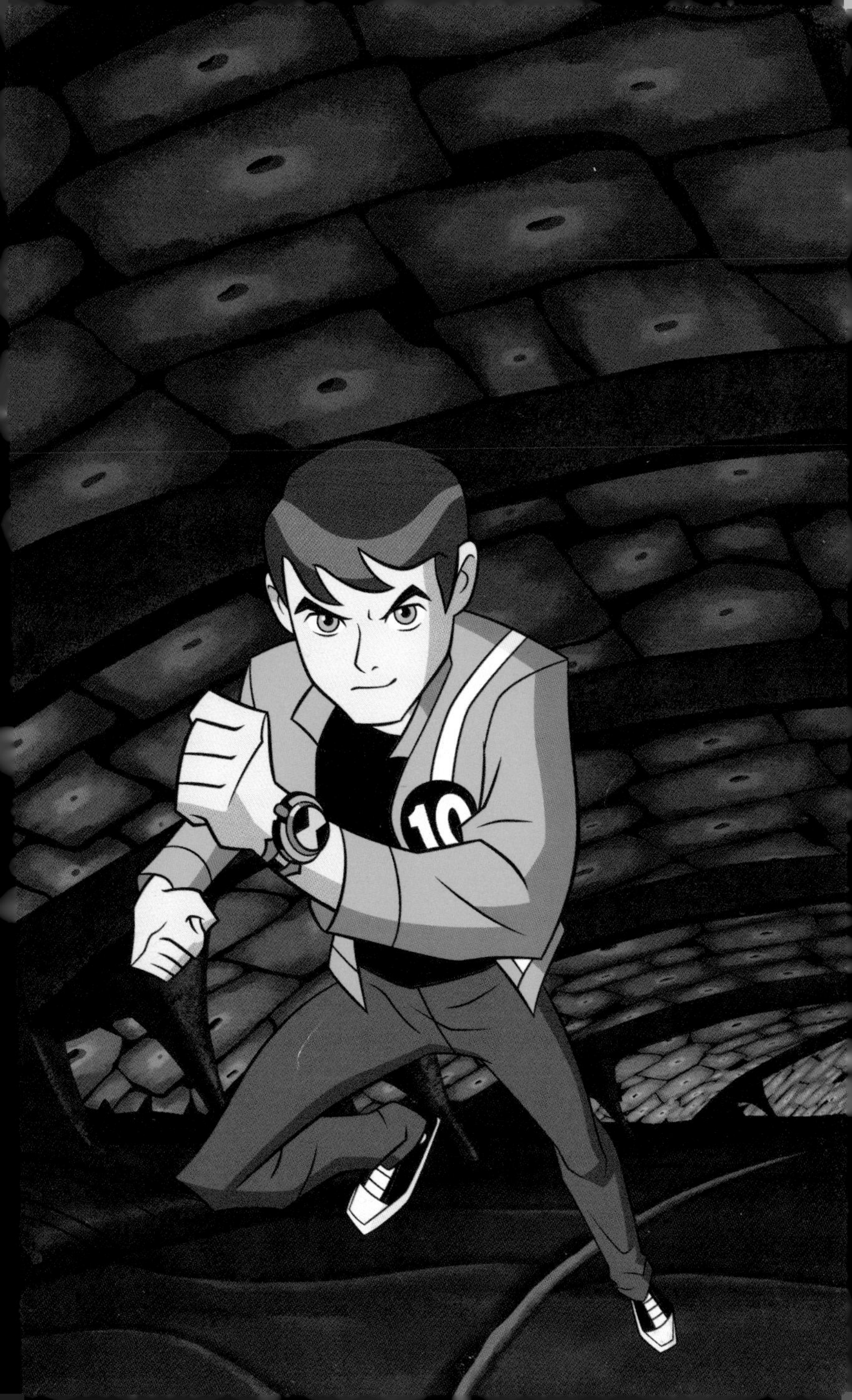
10

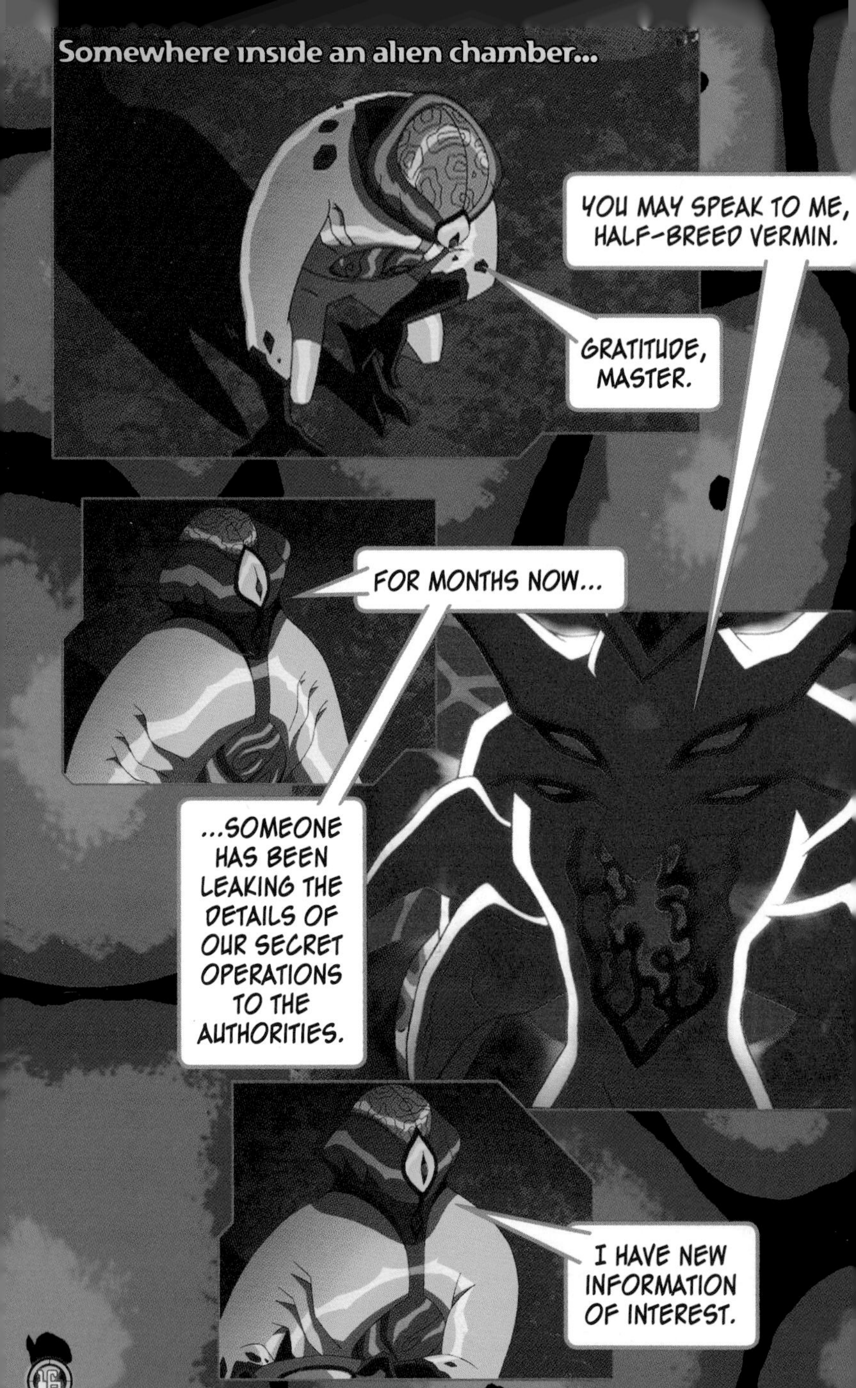
Somewhere inside an alien chamber...
GRATITUDE, MASTER.
YOU MAY SPEAK TO ME, HALF-BREED VERMIN.
FOR MONTHS NOW...
...SOMEONE HAS BEEN LEAKING THE DETAILS OF OUR SECRET OPERATIONS TO THE AUTHORITIES.
I HAVE NEW INFORMATION OF INTEREST.

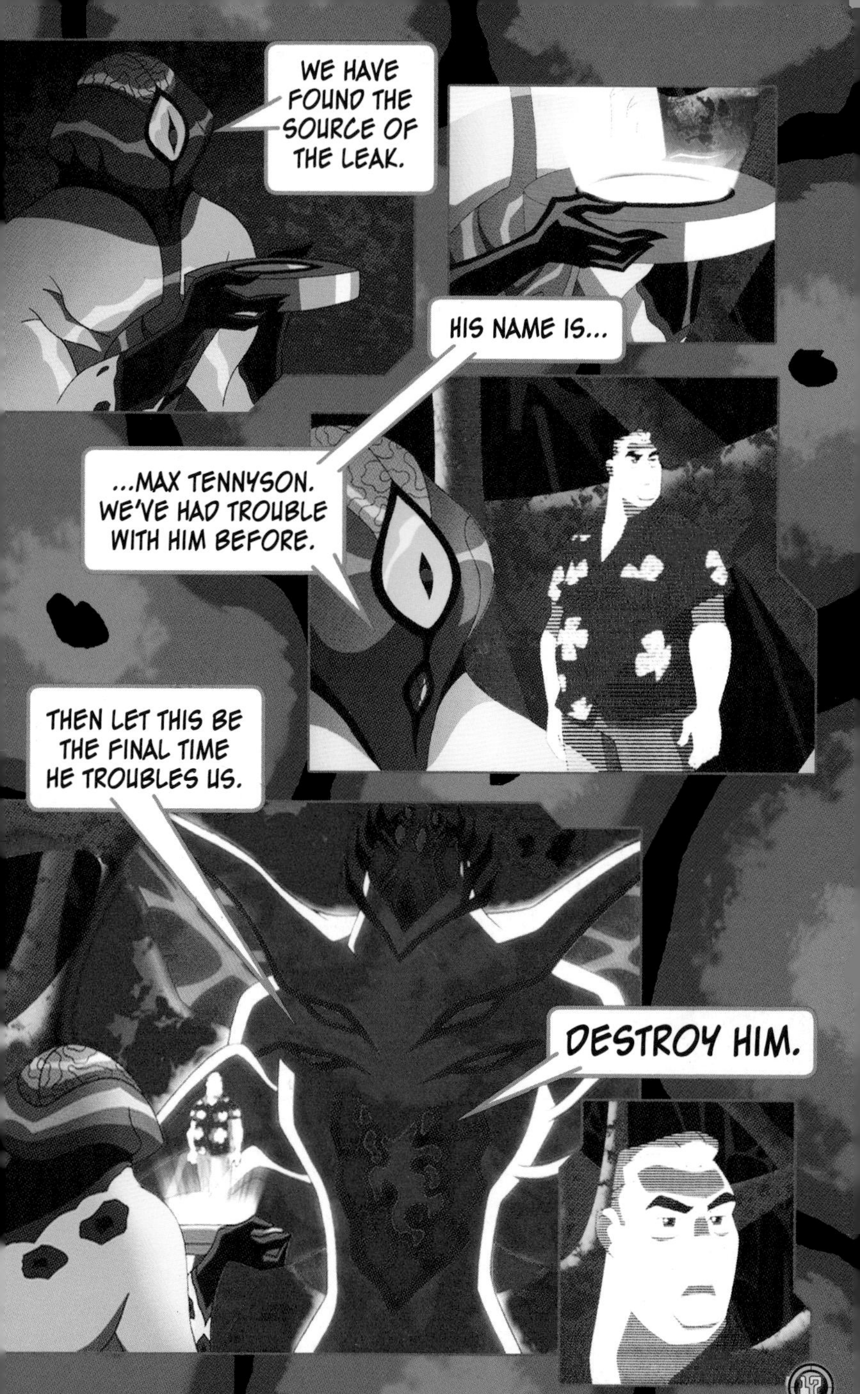
WE HAVE FOUND THE SOURCE OF THE LEAK.
HIS NAME IS...
...MAX TENNYSON. WE'VE HAD TROUBLE WITH HIM BEFORE.
THEN LET THIS BE THE FINAL TIME HE TROUBLES US.
DESTROY HIM.

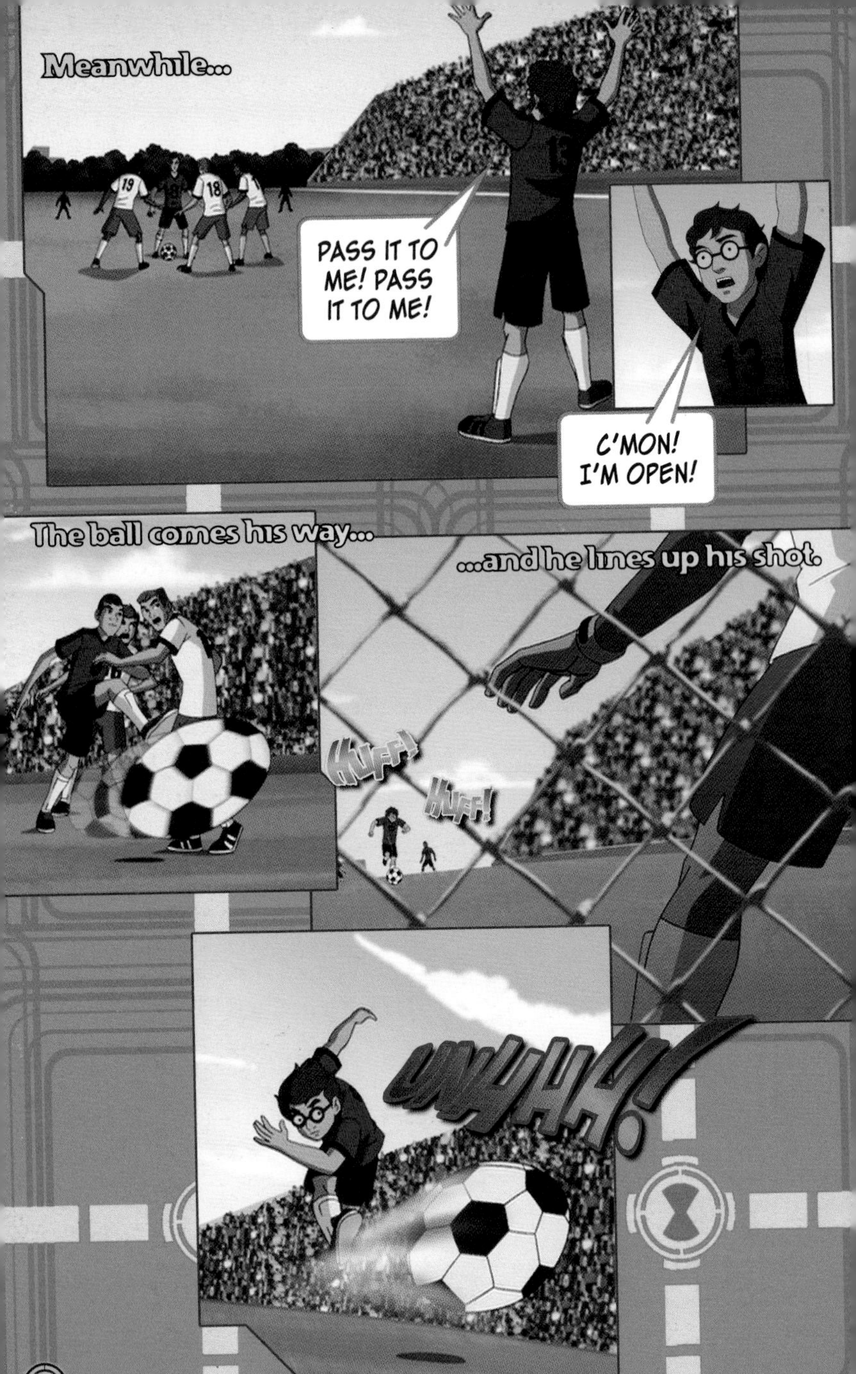
Meanwhile...
PASS IT TO ME! PASS IT TO ME!
C'MON! I'M OPEN!
The ball comes his way...
...and he lines up his shot.
HUFF!
HUFF!
UNHHH!

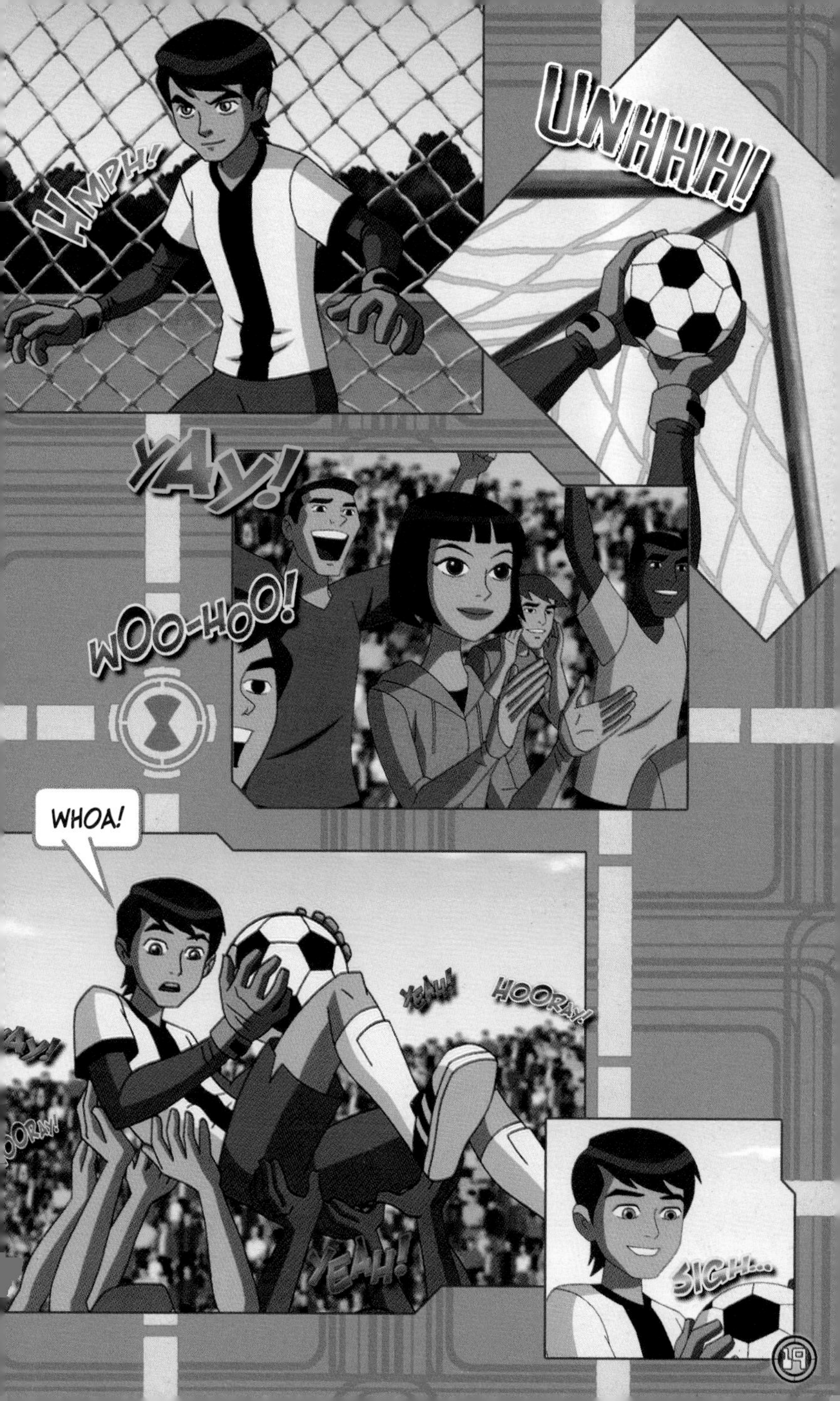
HMPH!
UNHHH!
YAY!
WOO-HOO!
WHOA!
YEAH!
HOORAY!
YEAH!
SIGH...

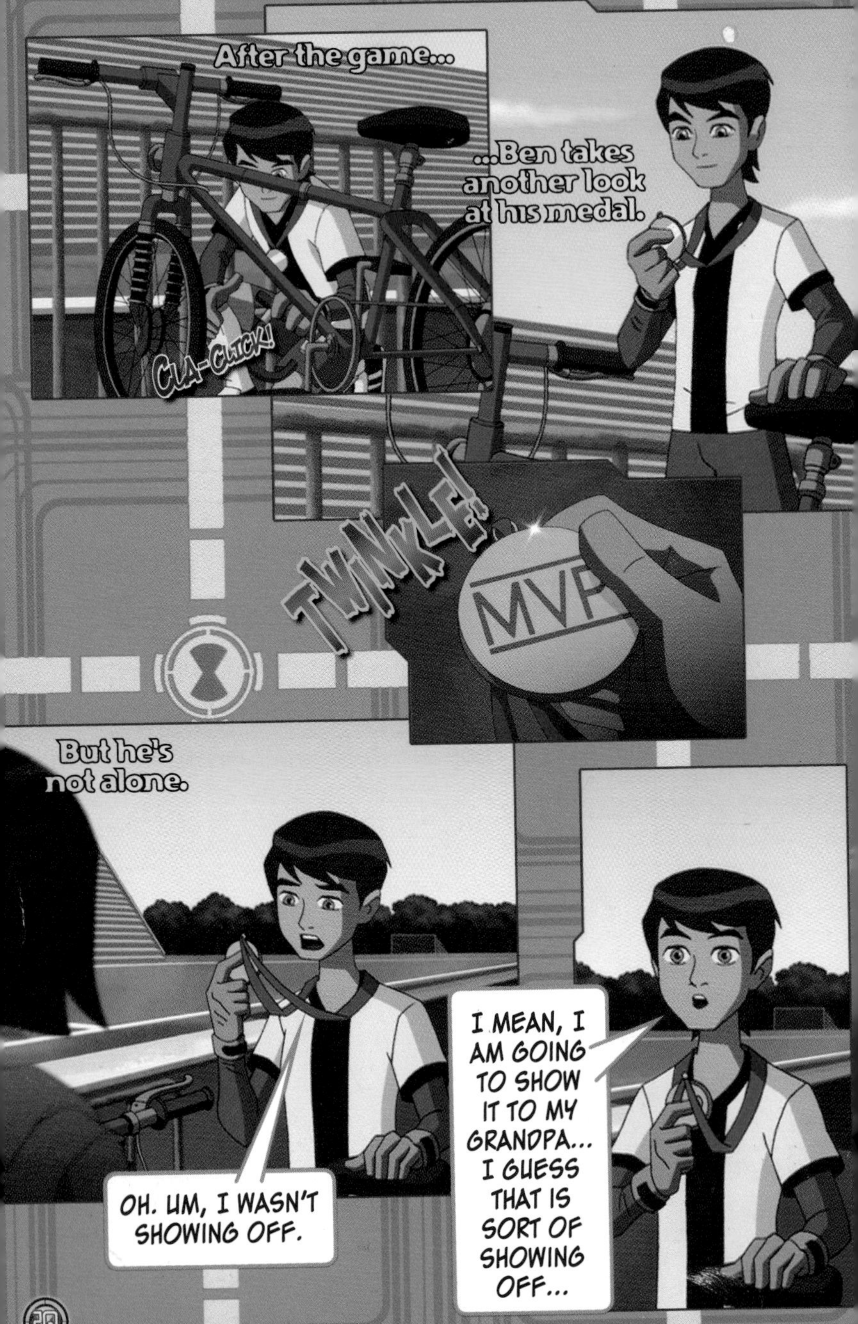
After the game...
CLA-CLICK!
...Ben takes another look at his medal.
TWINKLE!
MVP
But he's not alone.
OH. UM, I WASN'T SHOWING OFF.
I MEAN, I AM GOING TO SHOW IT TO MY GRANDPA... I GUESS THAT IS SORT OF SHOWING OFF...

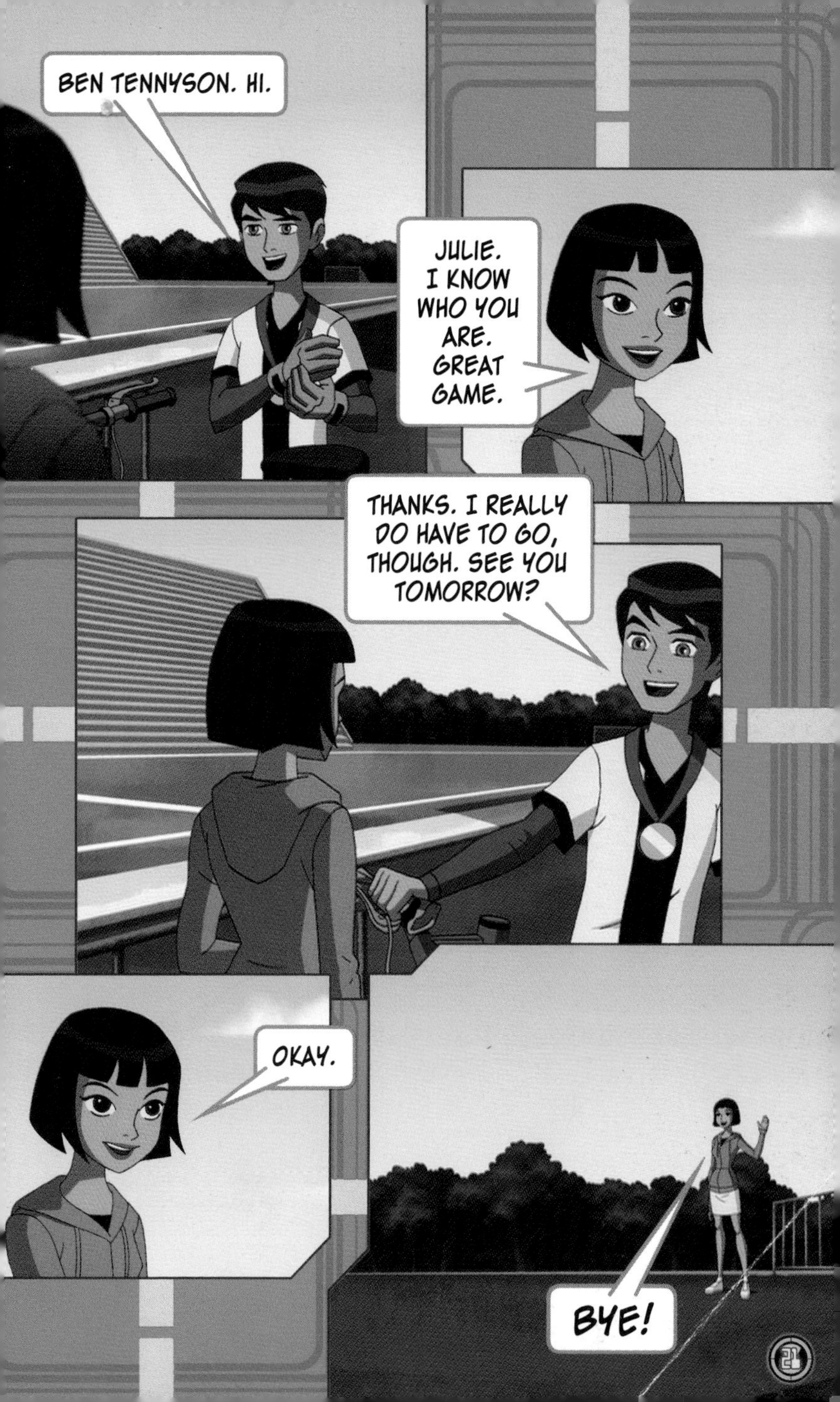
BEN TENNYSON. HI.
JULIE. I KNOW WHO YOU ARE. GREAT GAME.
THANKS. I REALLY DO HAVE TO GO, THOUGH. SEE YOU TOMORROW?
OKAY.
BYE!

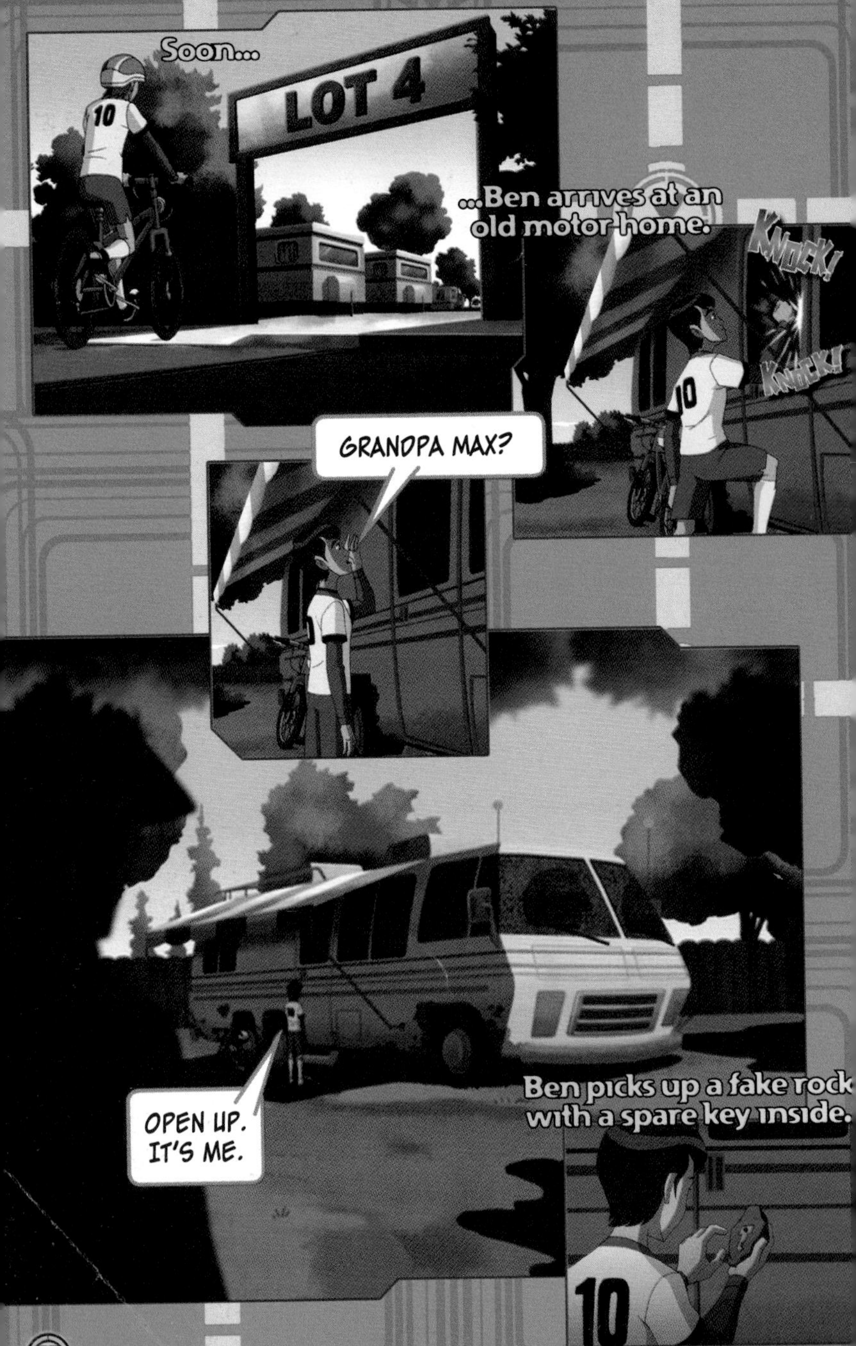

Soon...
LOT 4
...Ben arrives at an old motor home.
KNOCK!
KNOCK!
GRANDPA MAX?
OPEN UP. IT'S ME.
Ben picks up a fake rock with a spare key inside.

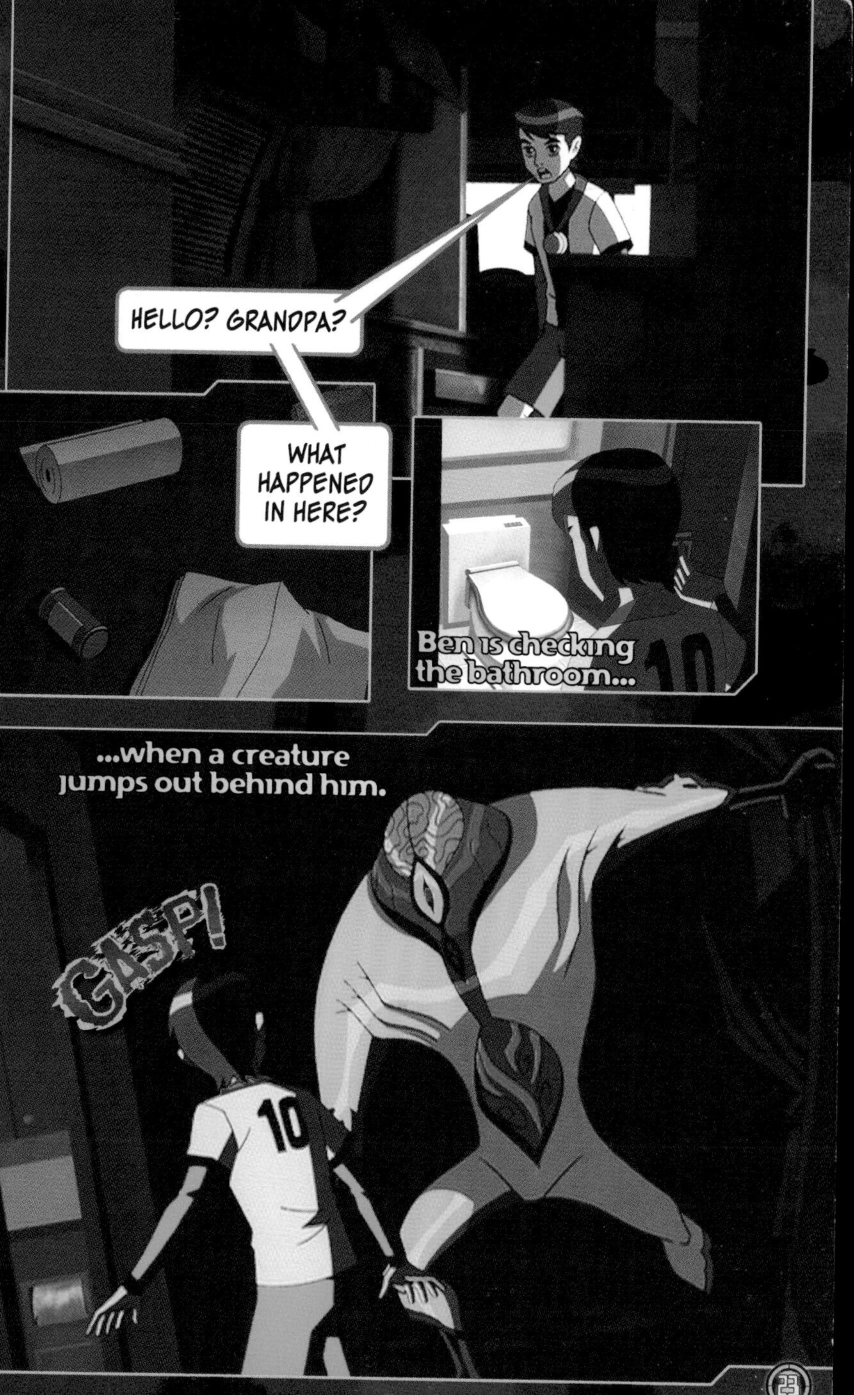
HELLO? GRANDPA?
WHAT HAPPENED IN HERE?
Ben is checking the bathroom...
...when a creature jumps out behind him.
GASP!

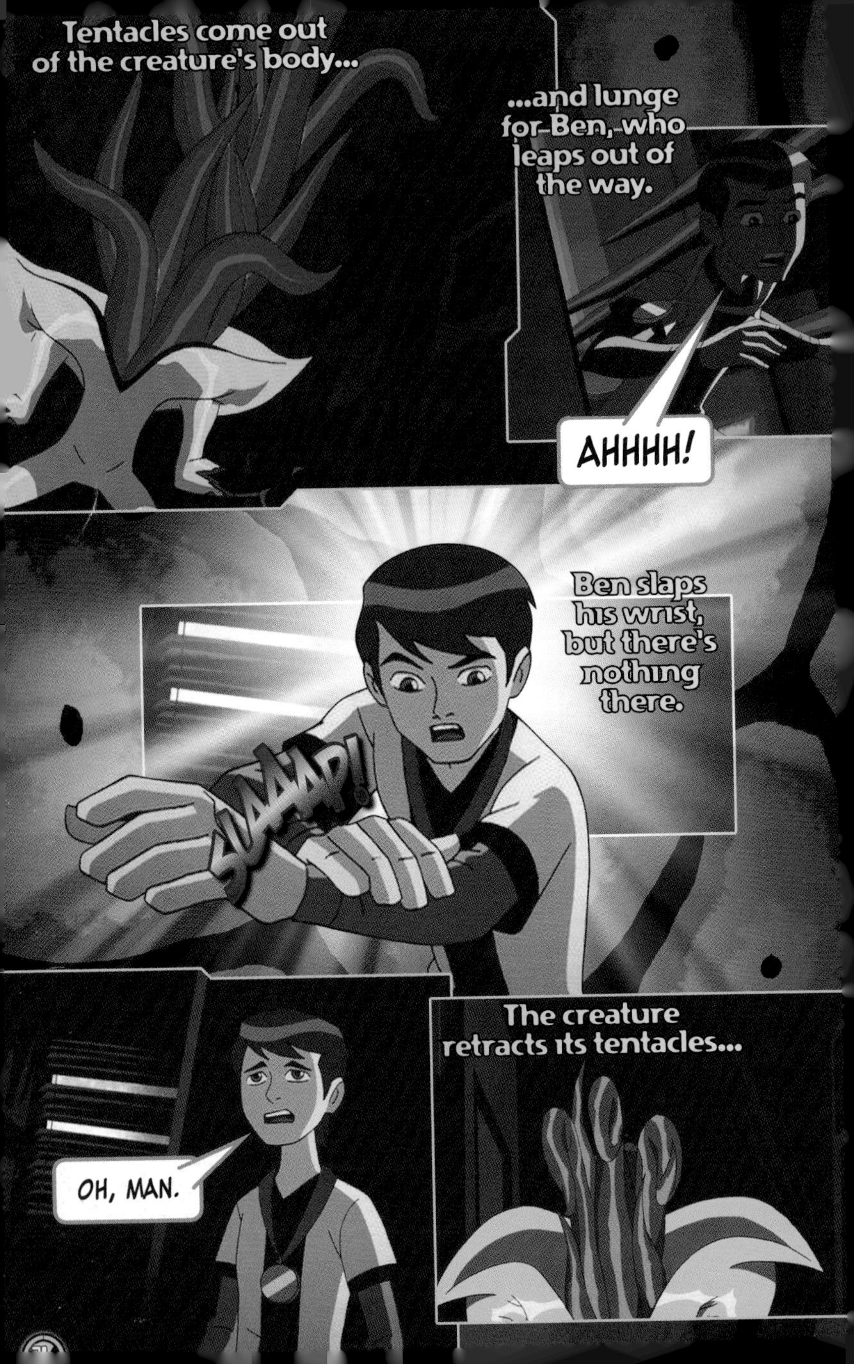
Tentacles come out of the creature's body...
...and lunge for Ben, who leaps out of the way.
AHHHH!
Ben slaps his wrist, but there's nothing there.
SLAAAP!
OH, MAN.
The creature retracts its tentacles...

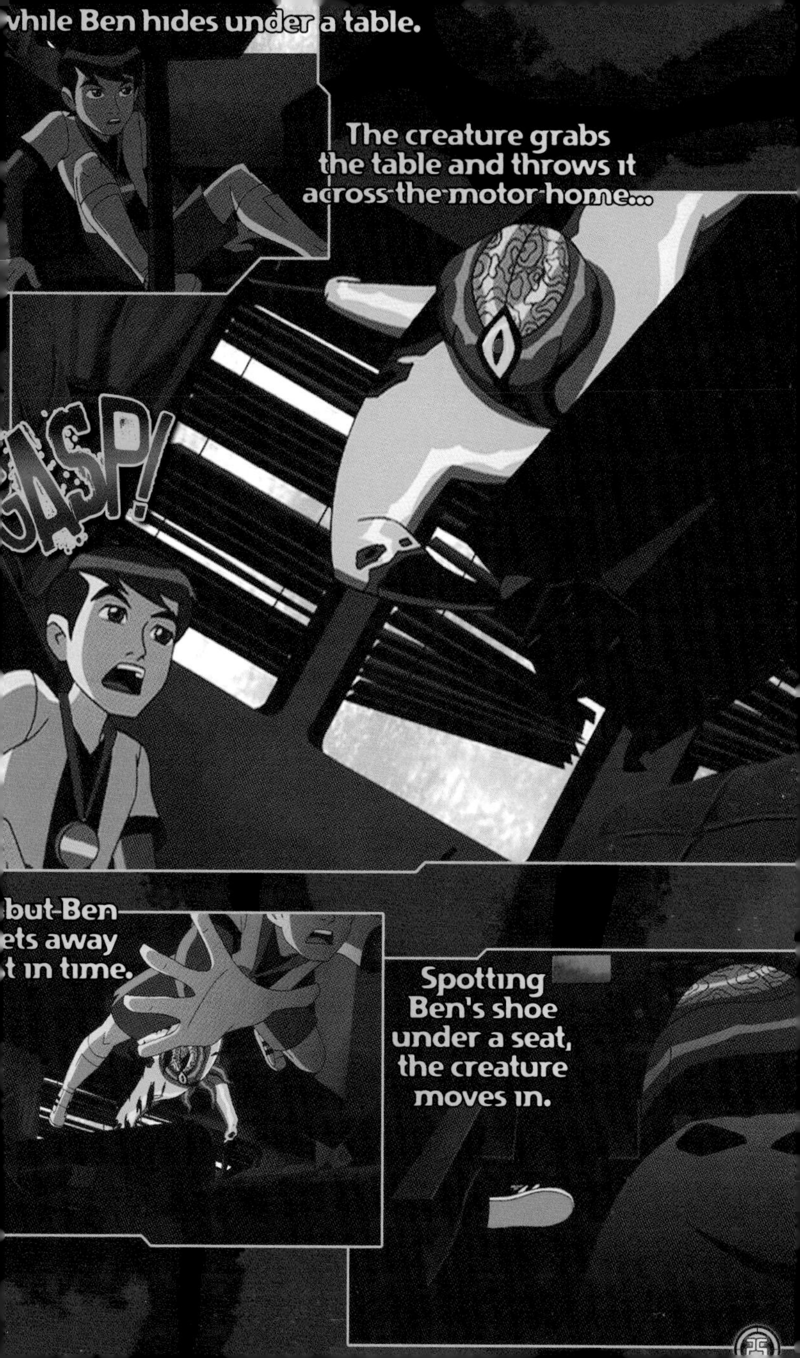
vhile Ben hides under a table.
The creature grabs the table and throws it across the motor home...
GASP!
but Ben
ets away
t in time.
Spotting Ben's shoe under a seat, the creature moves in.

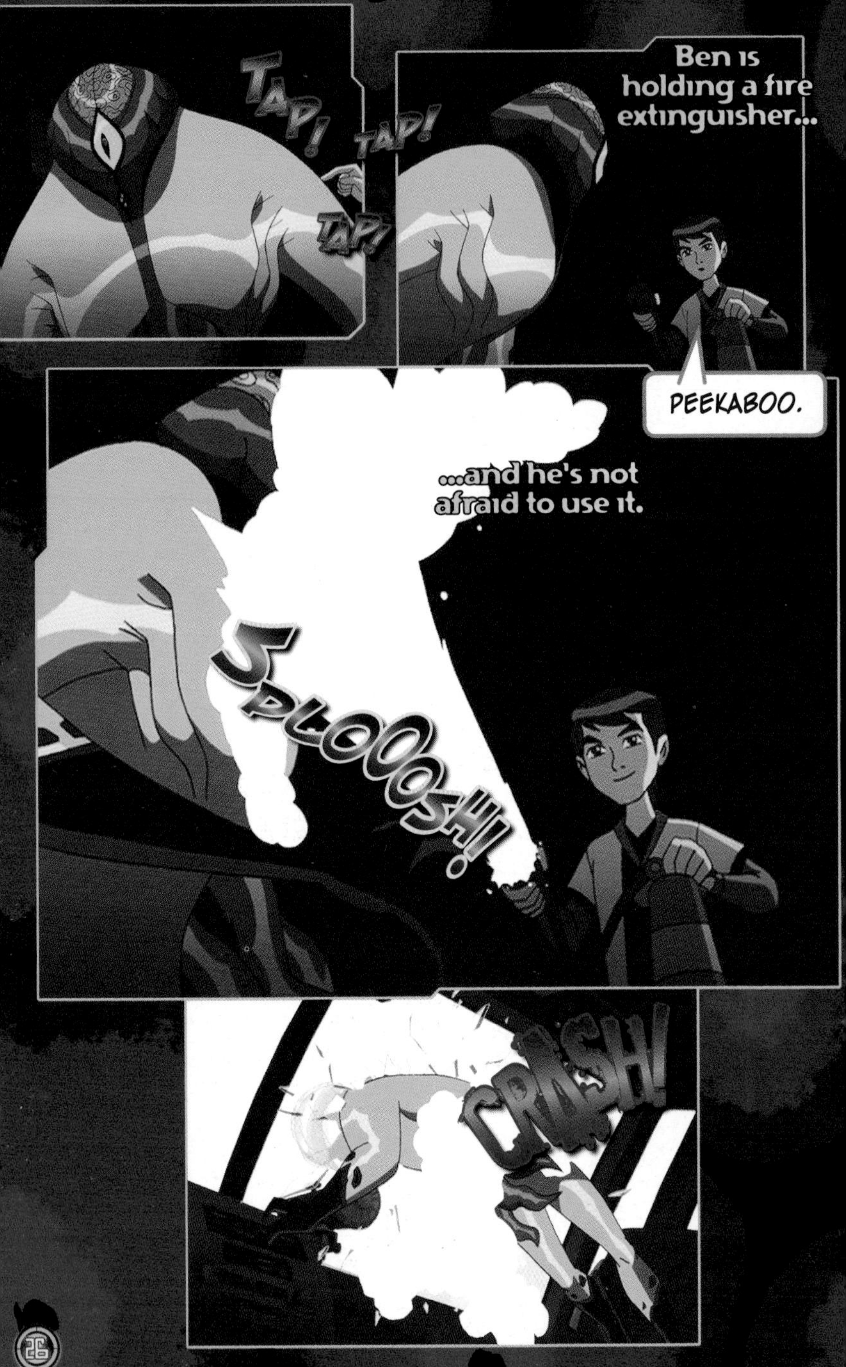
TAP! TAP!
TAP!
Ben is holding a fire extinguisher...
PEEKABOO.
...and he's not afraid to use it.
SPLOOOSH!!
CRASH!

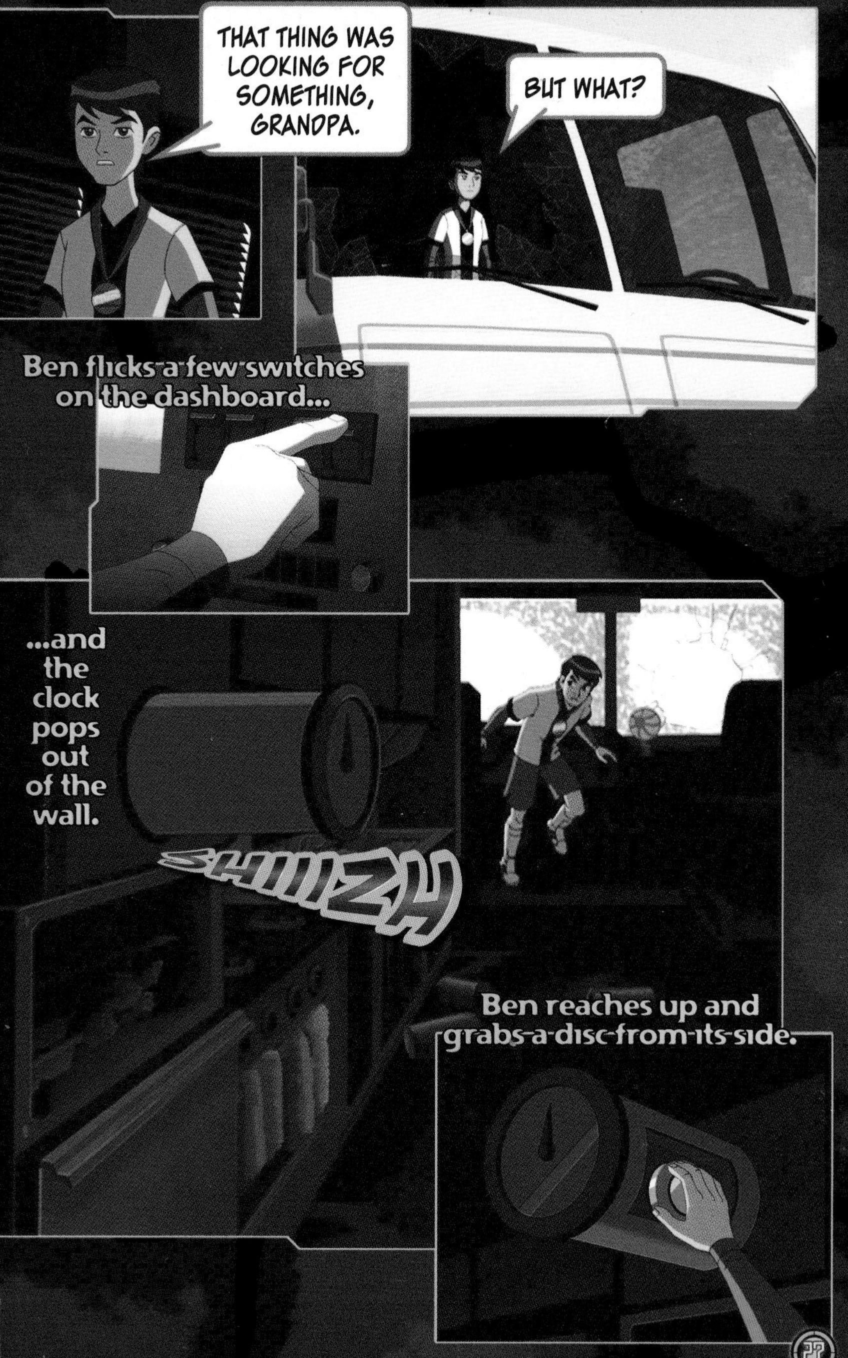
THAT THING WAS LOOKING FOR SOMETHING, GRANDPA.
BUT WHAT?
Ben flicks a few switches on the dashboard...
...and the clock pops out of the wall.
Ben reaches up and grabs a disc from its side.

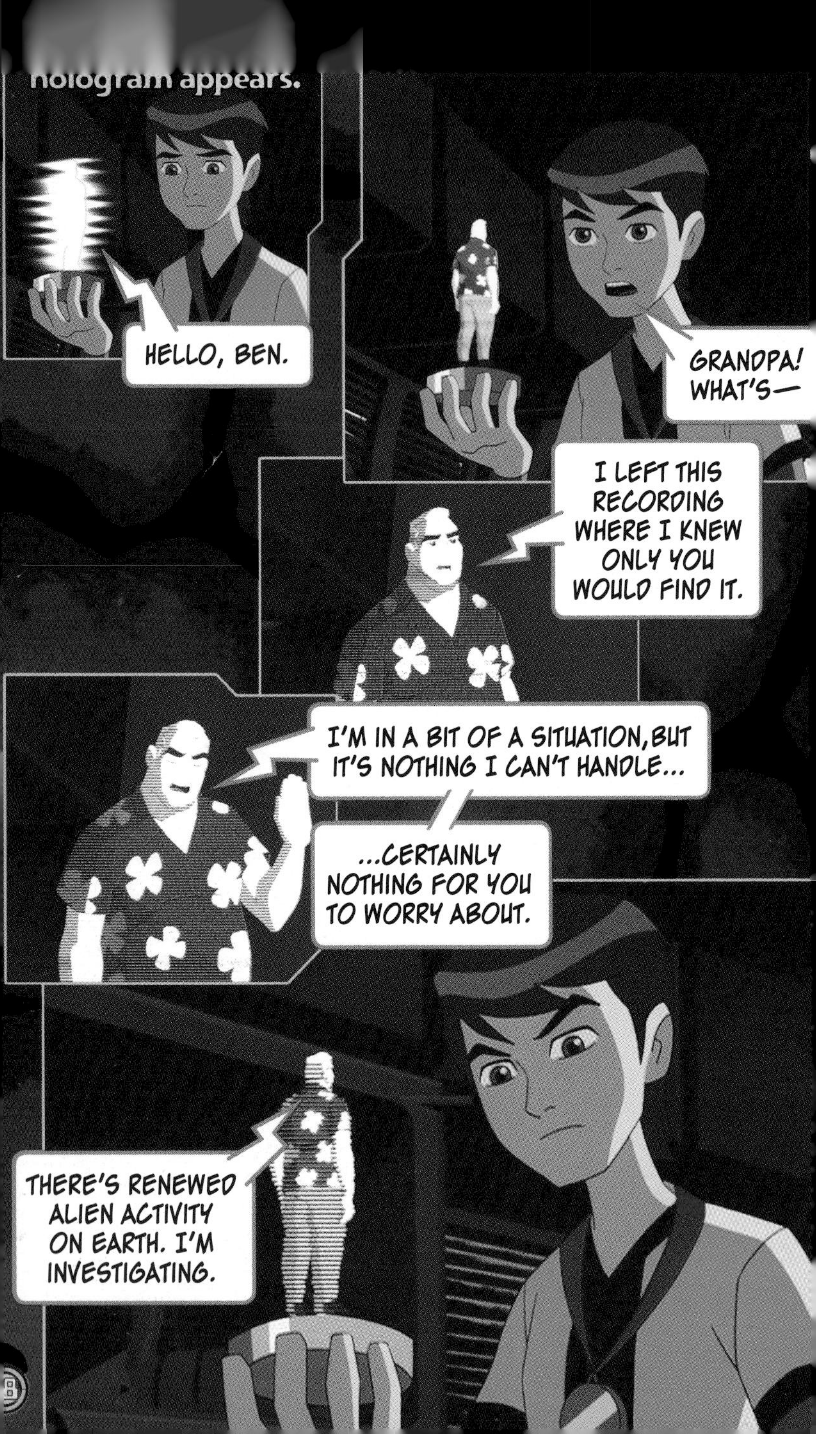
hologram appears.
HELLO, BEN.
GRANDPA! WHAT'S—
I LEFT THIS RECORDING WHERE I KNEW ONLY YOU WOULD FIND IT.
I'M IN A BIT OF A SITUATION, BUT IT'S NOTHING I CAN'T HANDLE...
...CERTAINLY NOTHING FOR YOU TO WORRY ABOUT.
THERE'S RENEWED ALIEN ACTIVITY ON EARTH. I'M INVESTIGATING.

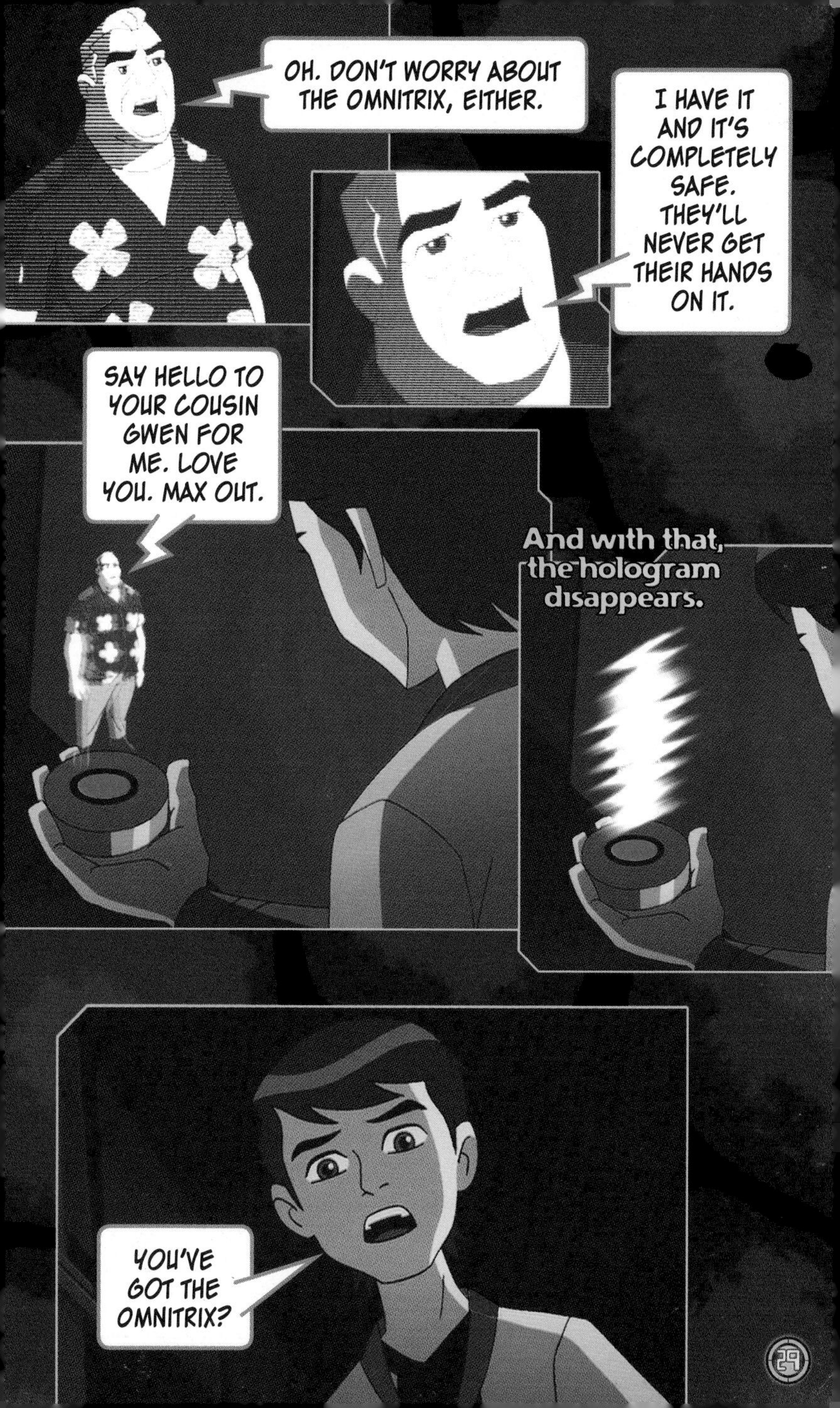

OH. DON'T WORRY ABOUT THE OMNITRIX, EITHER.
I HAVE IT AND IT'S COMPLETELY SAFE. THEY'LL NEVER GET THEIR HANDS ON IT.
SAY HELLO TO YOUR COUSIN GWEN FOR ME. LOVE YOU. MAX OUT.
And with that, the hologram disappears.
YOU'VE GOT THE OMNITRIX?

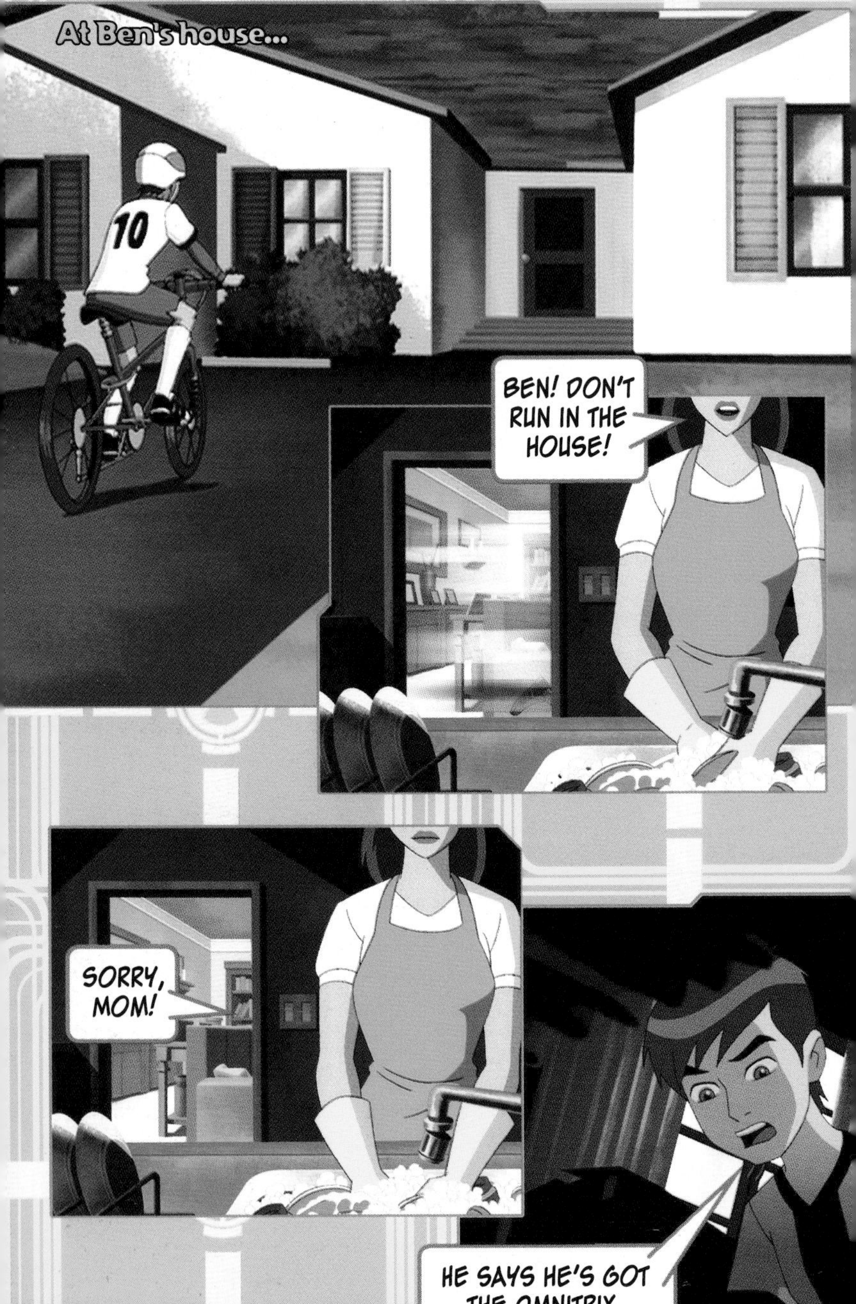
At Ben's house...
BEN! DON'T RUN IN THE HOUSE!
SORRY, MOM!
HE SAYS HE'S GOT THE OMNITRIX.

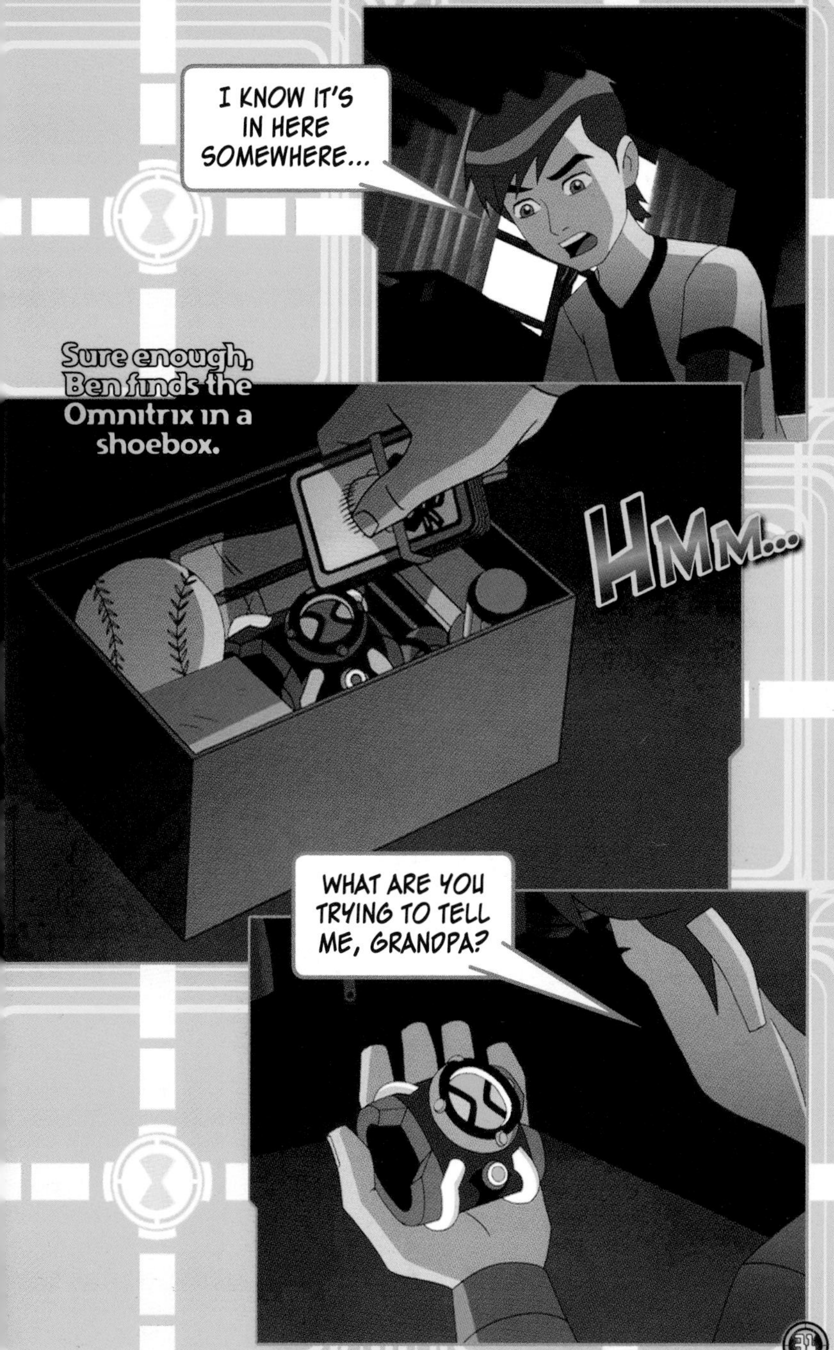
I KNOW IT'S IN HERE SOMEWHERE...
Sure enough, Ben finds the Omnitrix in a shoebox.
HMM...
WHAT ARE YOU TRYING TO TELL ME, GRANDPA?

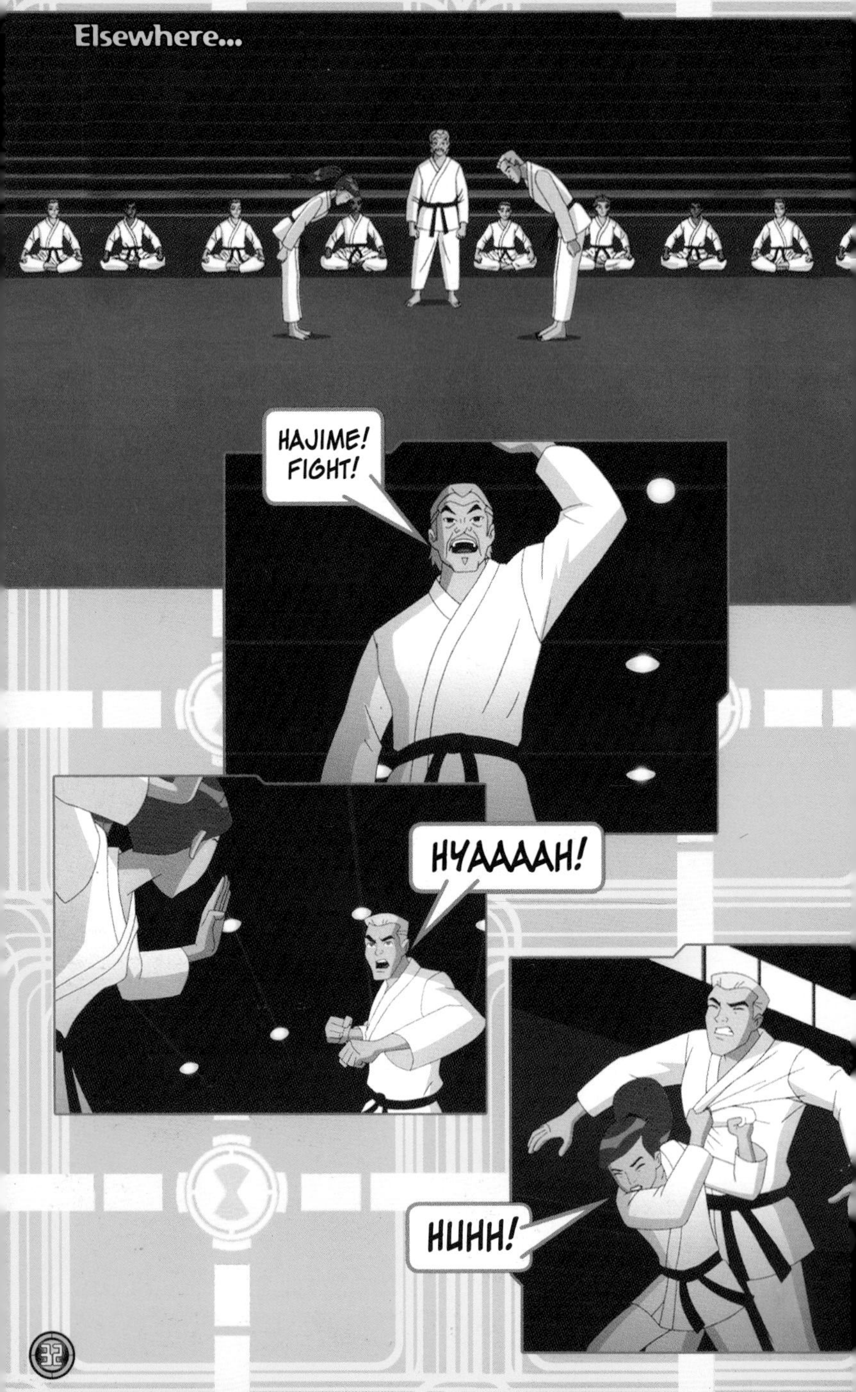
Elsewhere...
HAJIME! FIGHT!
HYAAAAH!
HUHH!

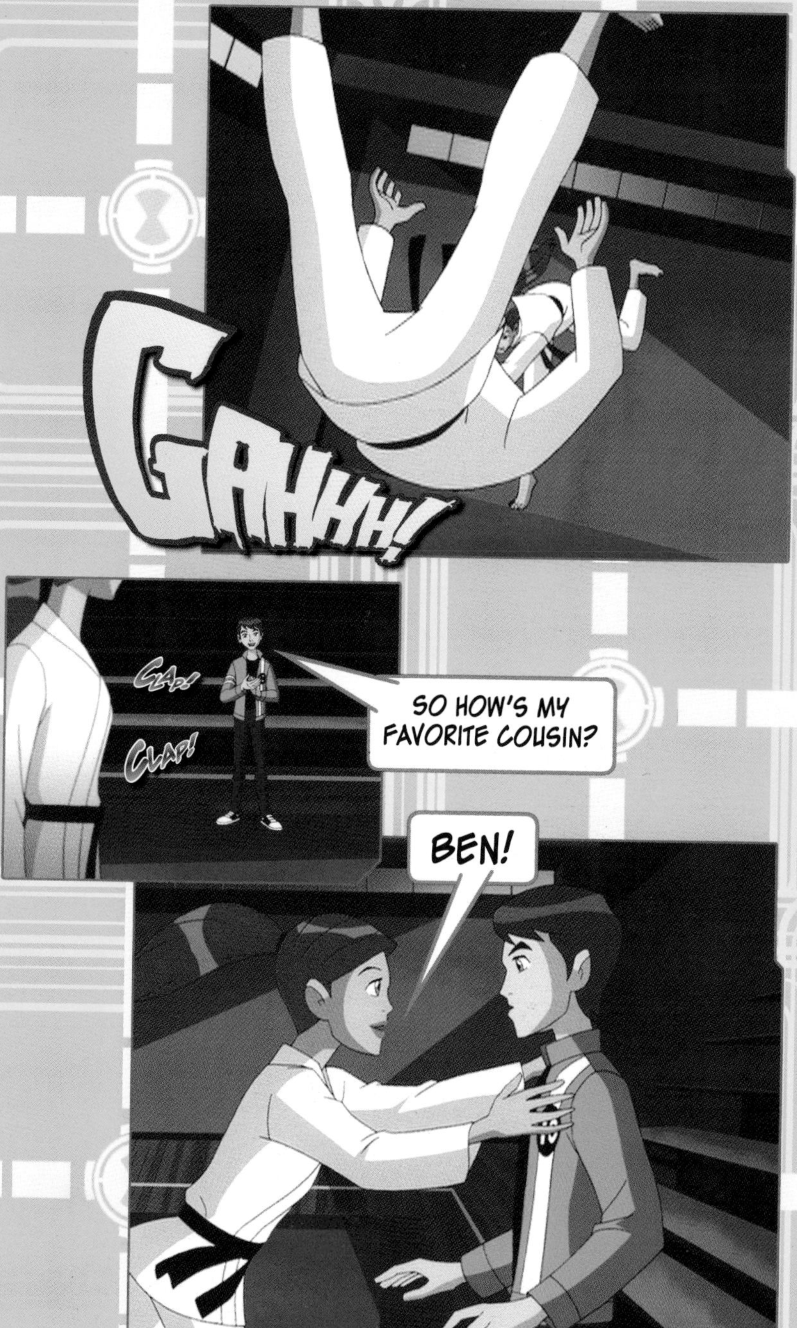
GAHHH!
CLAP!
CLAP!
SO HOW'S MY FAVORITE COUSIN?
BEN!

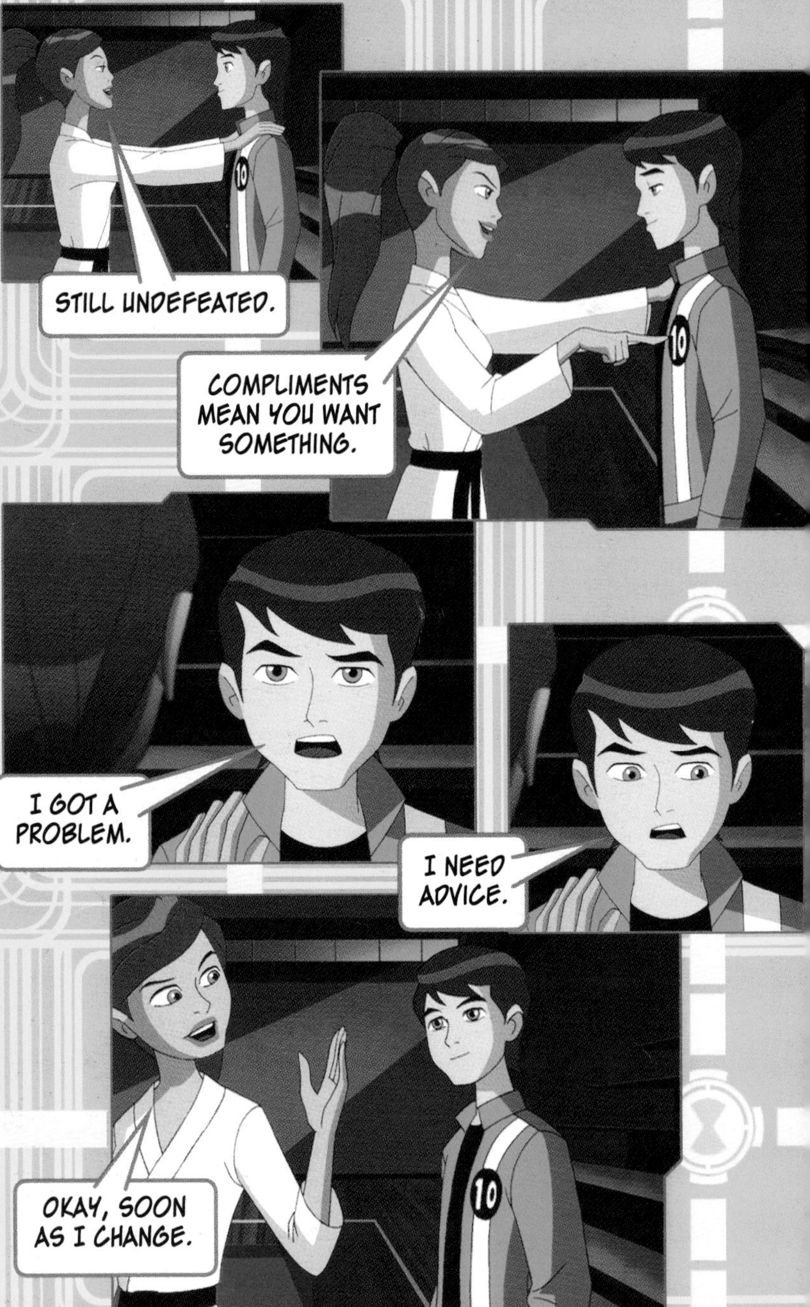
STILL UNDEFEATED.
COMPLIMENTS MEAN YOU WANT SOMETHING.
I GOT A PROBLEM.
I NEED ADVICE.
OKAY, SOON AS I CHANGE.

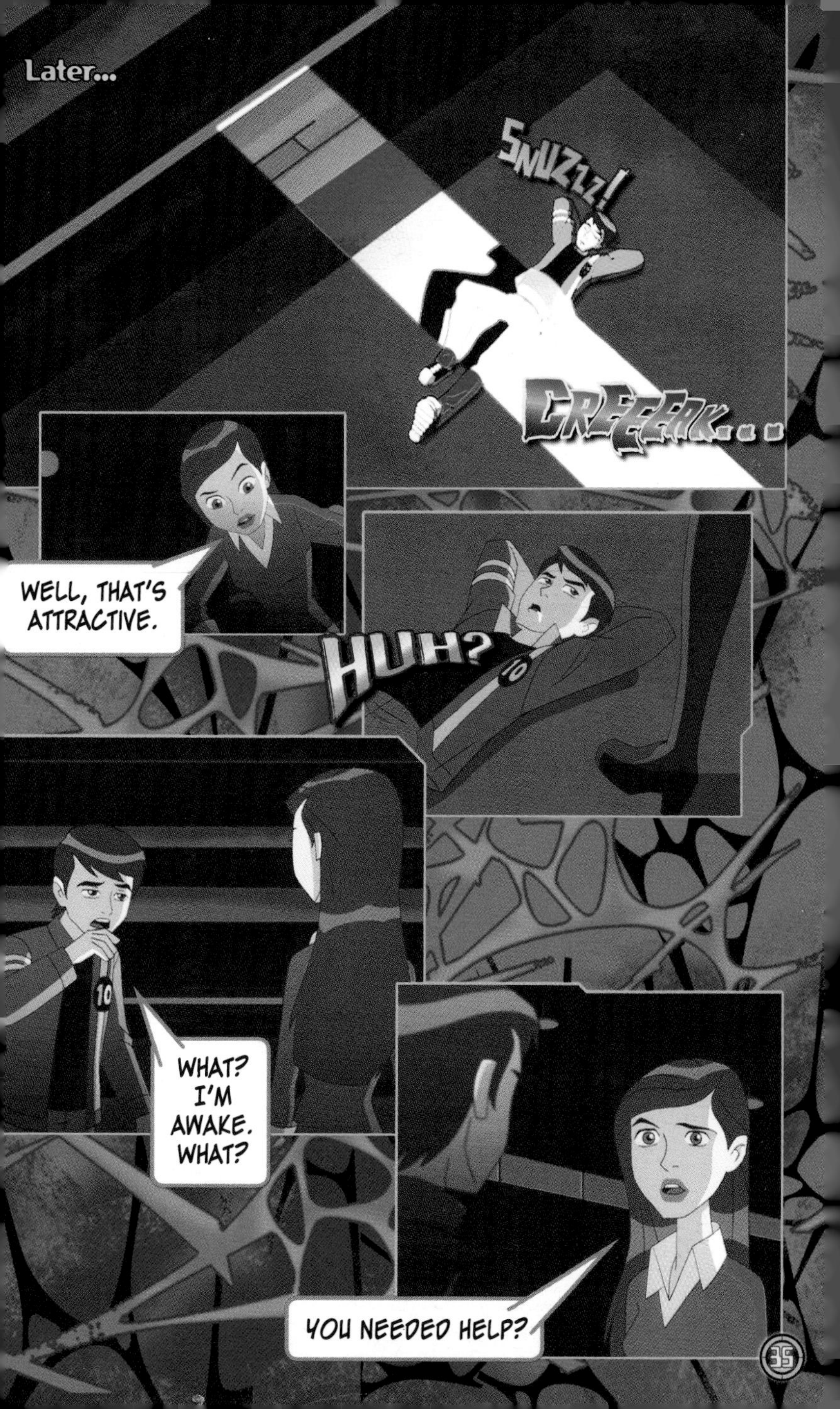

Later...
SNUZzz!
CREEEAK...
WELL, THAT'S ATTRACTIVE.
HUH?
WHAT? I'M AWAKE. WHAT?
YOU NEEDED HELP?

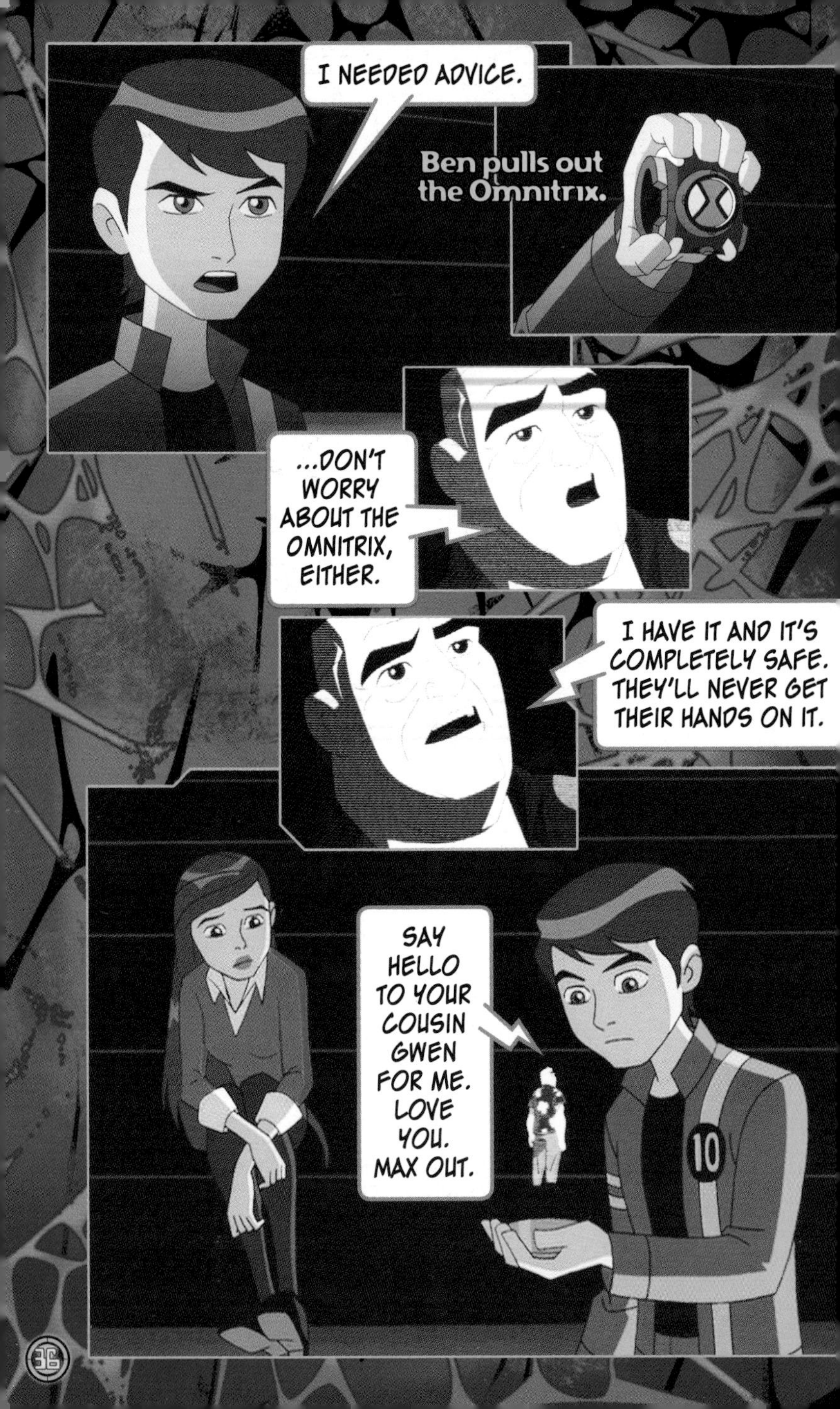

I NEEDED ADVICE.
Ben pulls out the Omnitrix.
...DON'T WORRY ABOUT THE OMNITRIX, EITHER.
I HAVE IT AND IT'S COMPLETELY SAFE. THEY'LL NEVER GET THEIR HANDS ON IT.
SAY HELLO TO YOUR COUSIN GWEN FOR ME. LOVE YOU. MAX OUT.

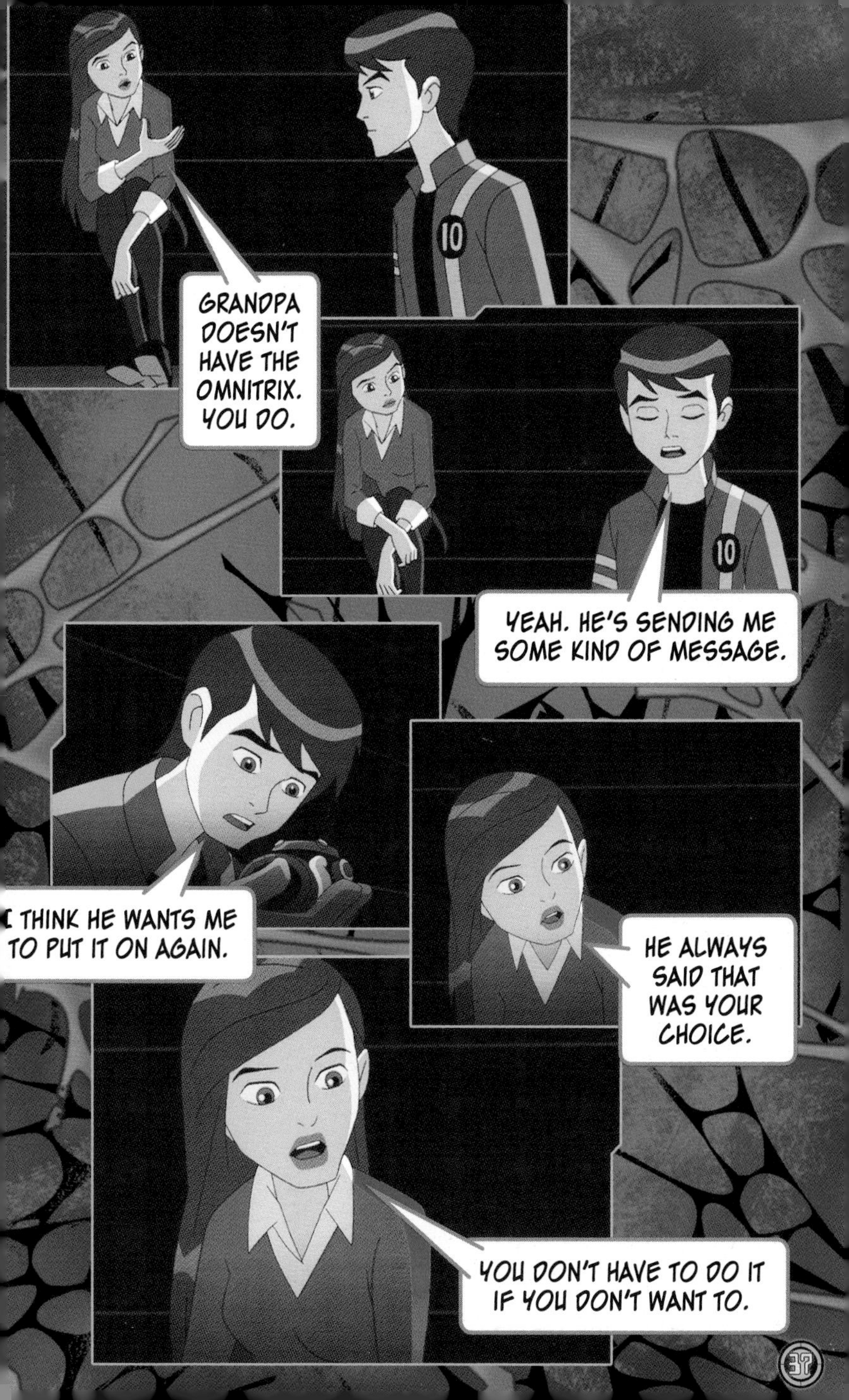
GRANDPA DOESN'T HAVE THE OMNITRIX. YOU DO.
YEAH. HE'S SENDING ME SOME KIND OF MESSAGE.
I THINK HE WANTS ME TO PUT IT ON AGAIN.
HE ALWAYS SAID THAT WAS YOUR CHOICE.
YOU DON'T HAVE TO DO IT IF YOU DON'T WANT TO.

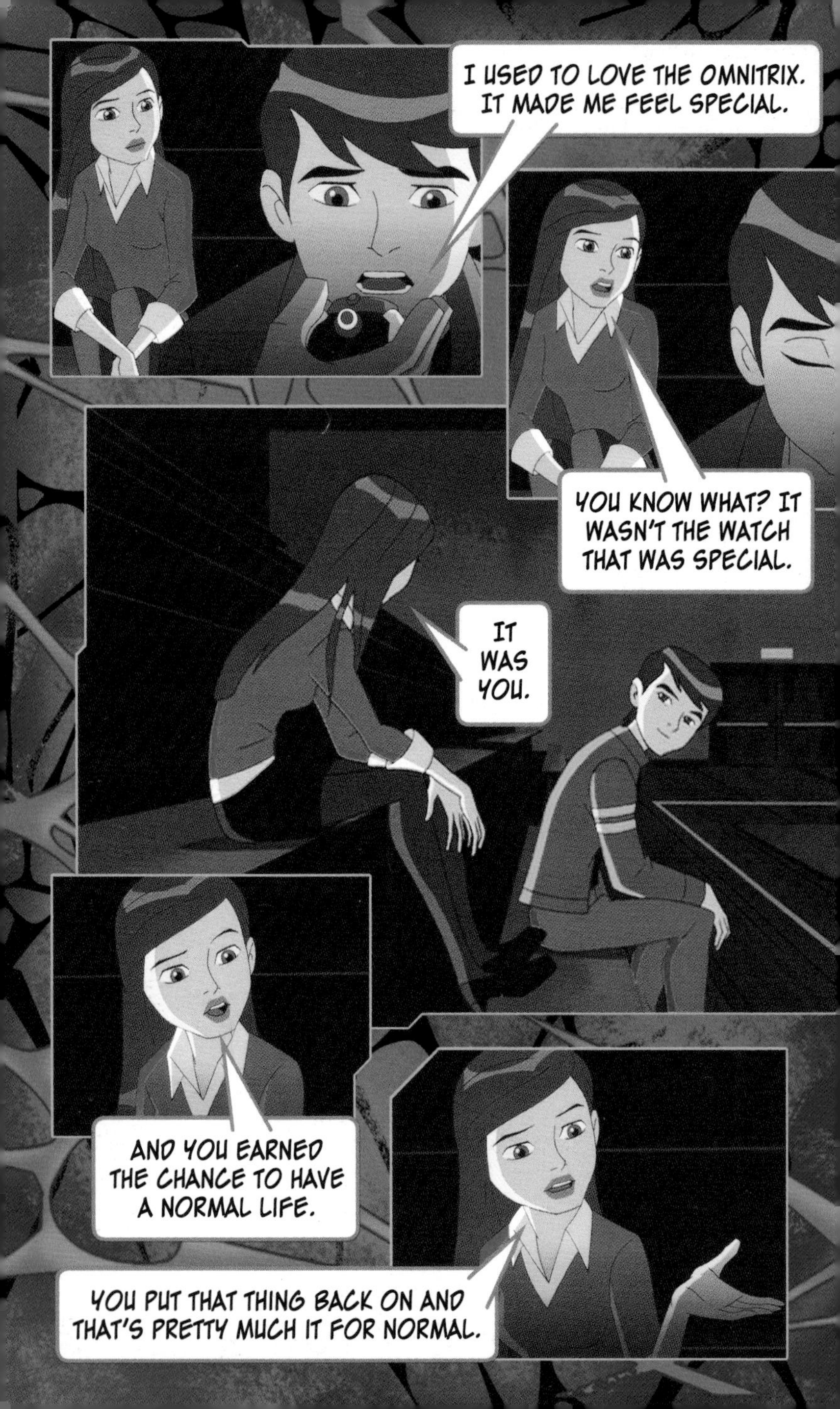
I USED TO LOVE THE OMNITRIX. IT MADE ME FEEL SPECIAL.
YOU KNOW WHAT? IT WASN'T THE WATCH THAT WAS SPECIAL.
IT WAS YOU.
AND YOU EARNED THE CHANCE TO HAVE A NORMAL LIFE.
YOU PUT THAT THING BACK ON AND THAT'S PRETTY MUCH IT FOR NORMAL.

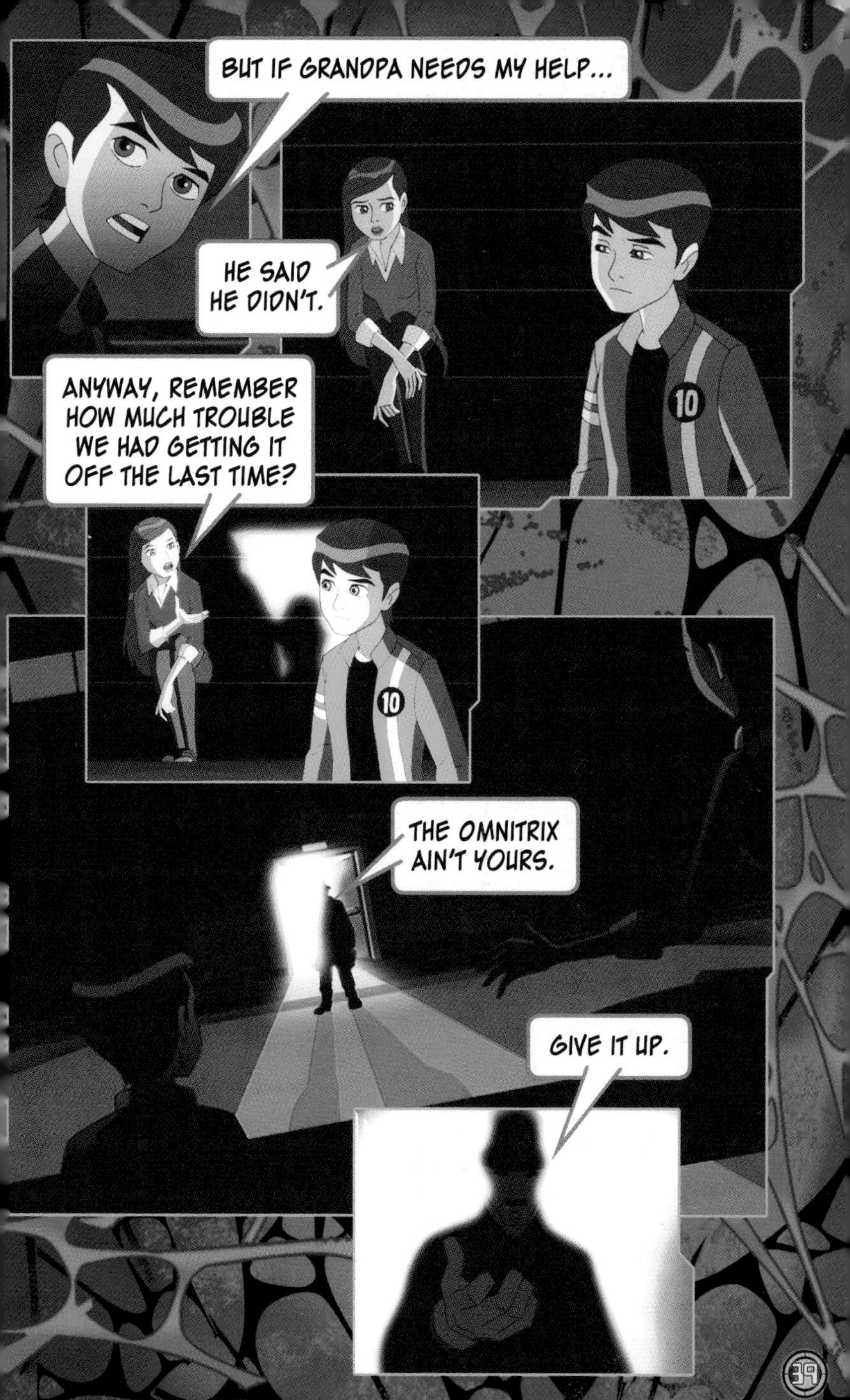
BUT IF GRANDPA NEEDS MY HELP...
HE SAID HE DIDN'T.
ANYWAY, REMEMBER HOW MUCH TROUBLE WE HAD GETTING IT OFF THE LAST TIME?
THE OMNITRIX AIN'T YOURS.
GIVE IT UP.

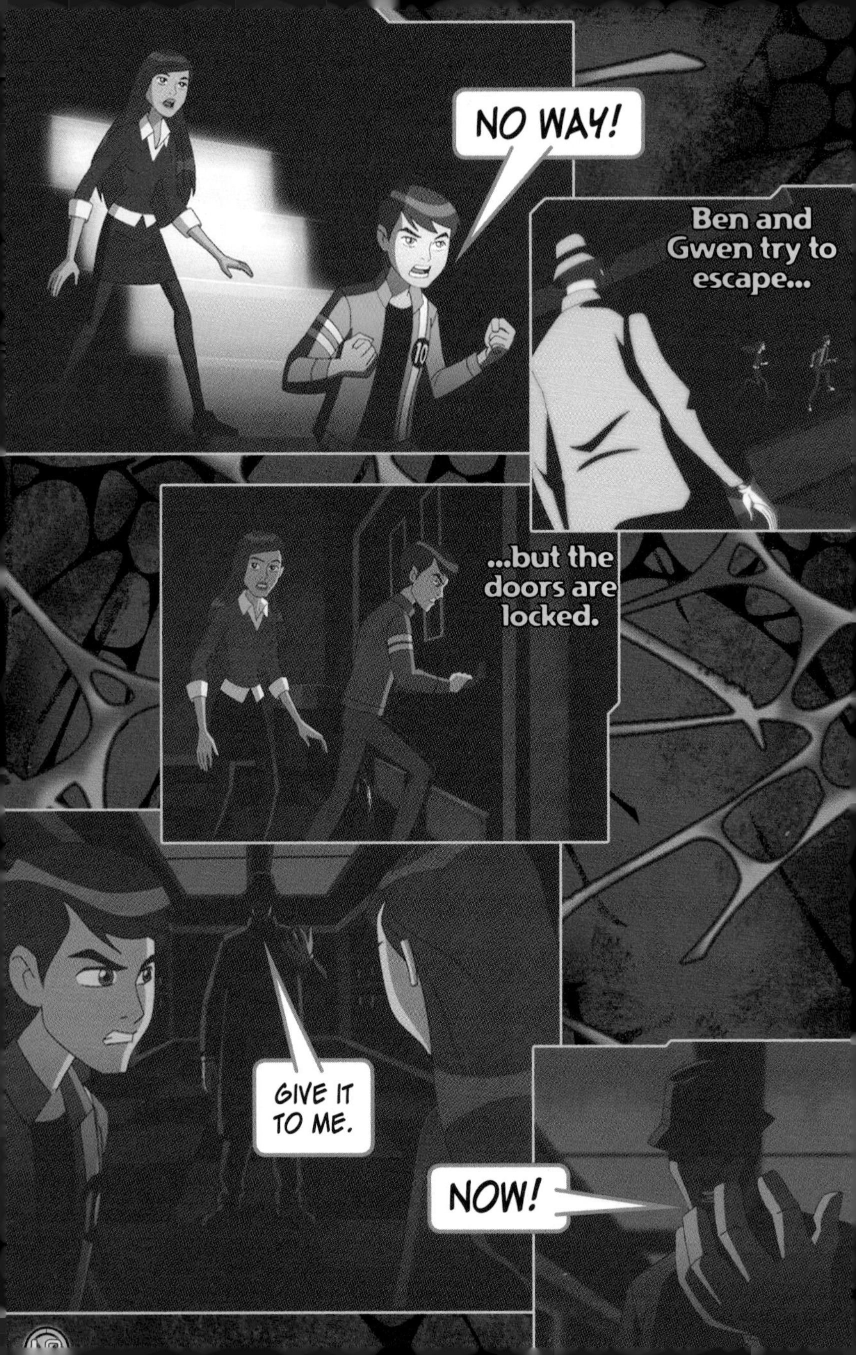
NO WAY!
Ben and Gwen try to escape...
...but the doors are locked.
GIVE IT TO ME.
NOW!

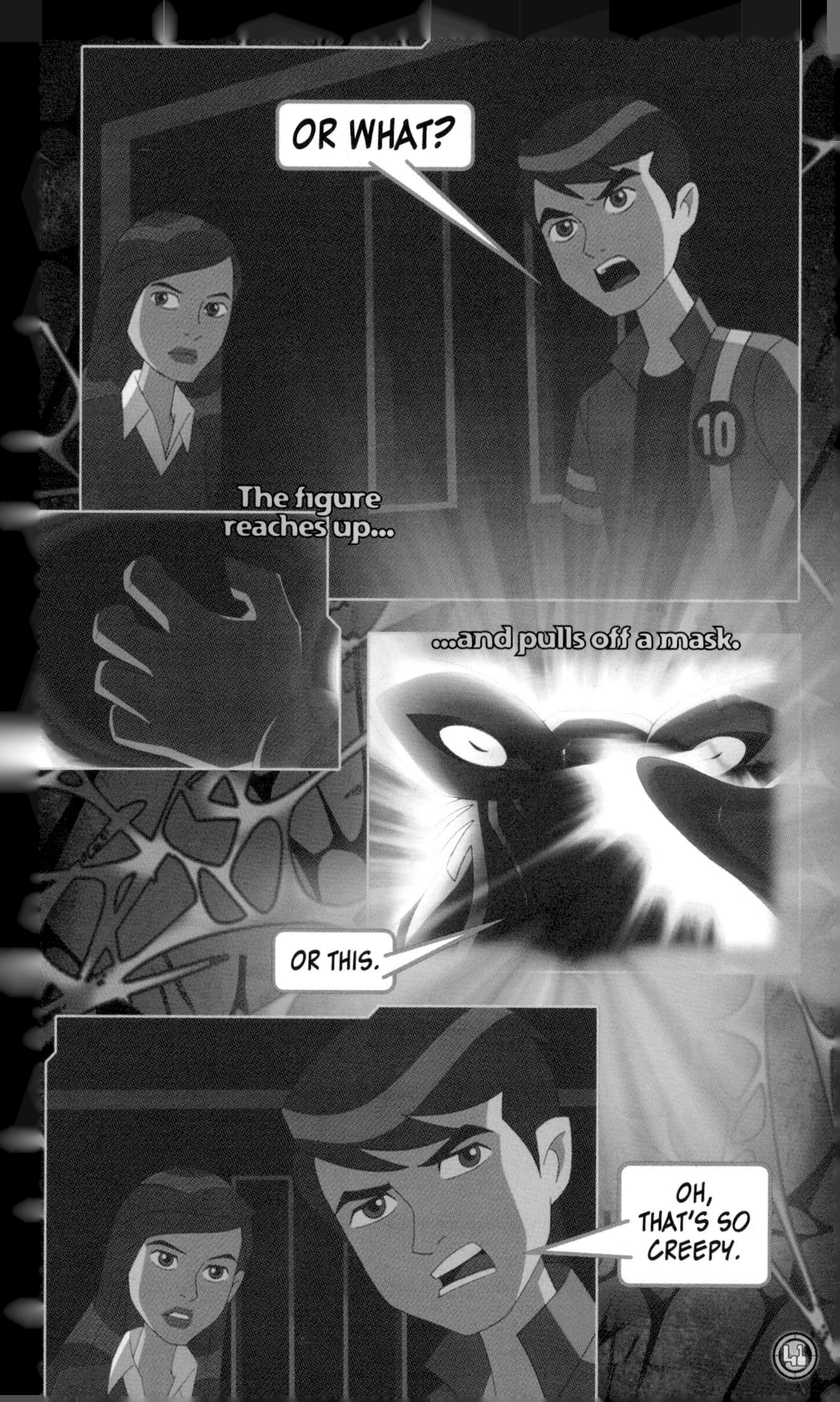
OR WHAT?
The figure reaches up...
...and pulls off a mask.
OR THIS.
OH, THAT'S SO CREEPY.

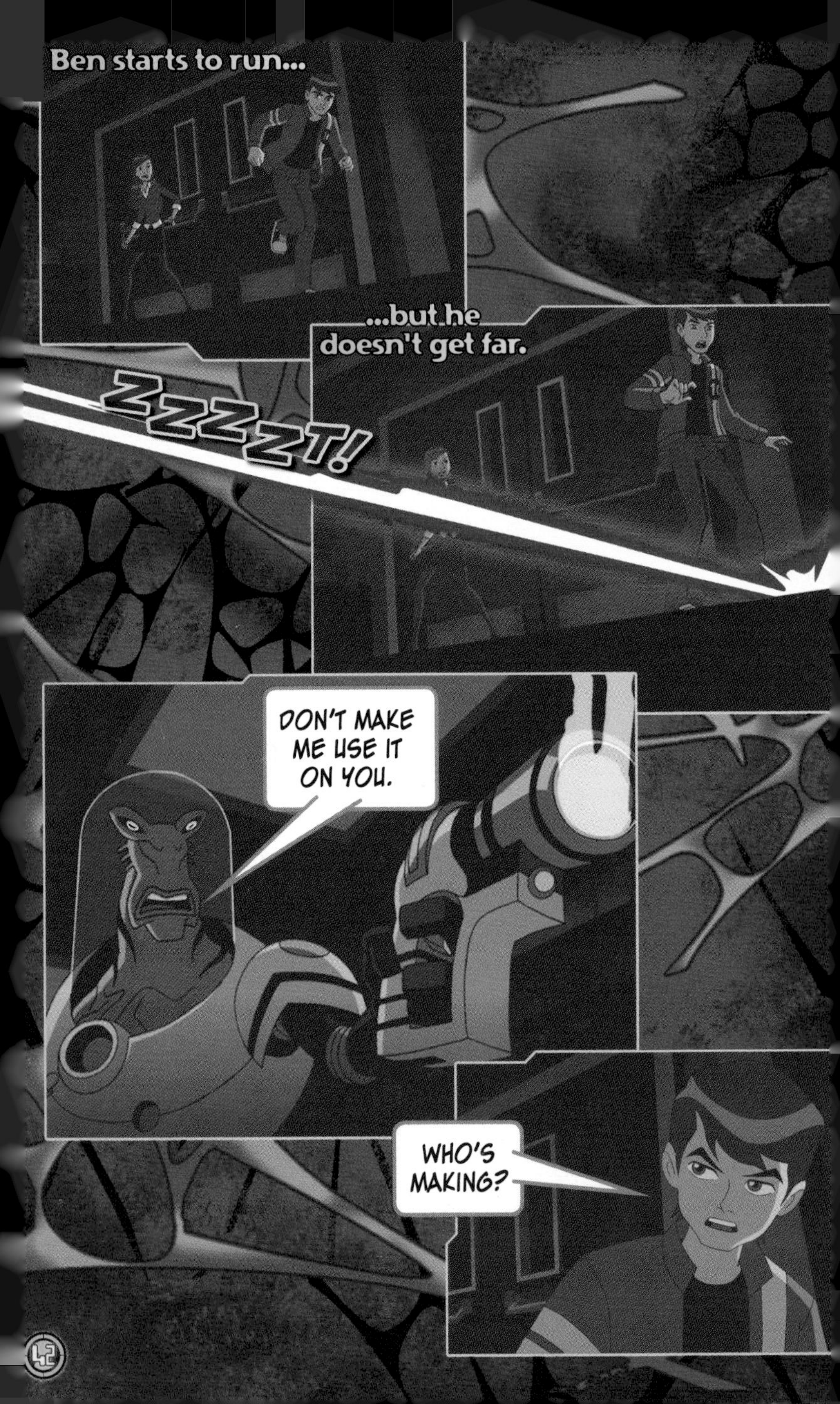
Ben starts to run...
...but he doesn't get far.
ZZZZT!
DON'T MAKE ME USE IT ON YOU.
WHO'S MAKING?

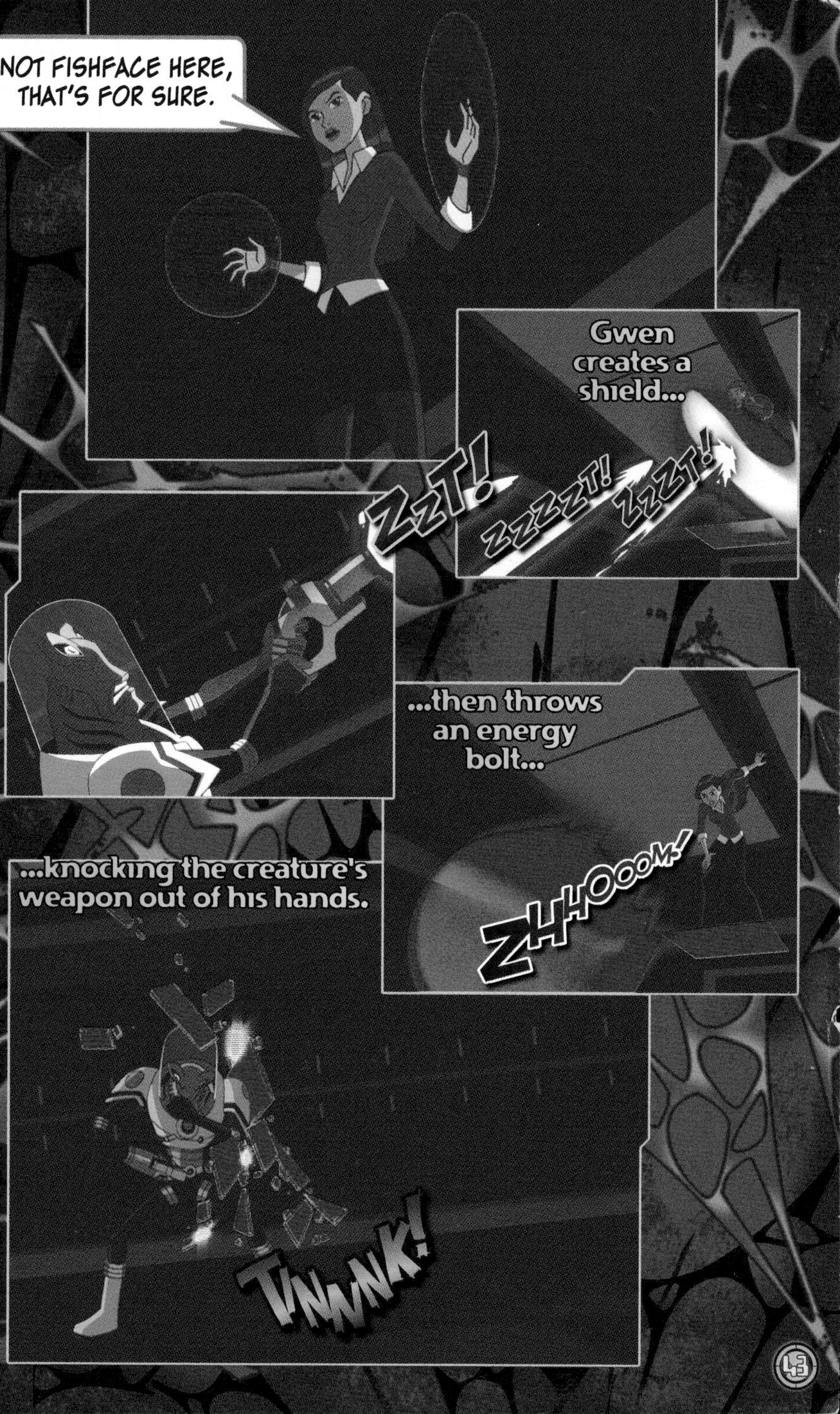
NOT FISHFACE HERE, THAT'S FOR SURE.
Gwen creates a shield...
ZzT!
ZZZZT!
ZZZT!
...then throws an energy bolt...
ZHHOOOM!
...knocking the creature's weapon out of his hands.

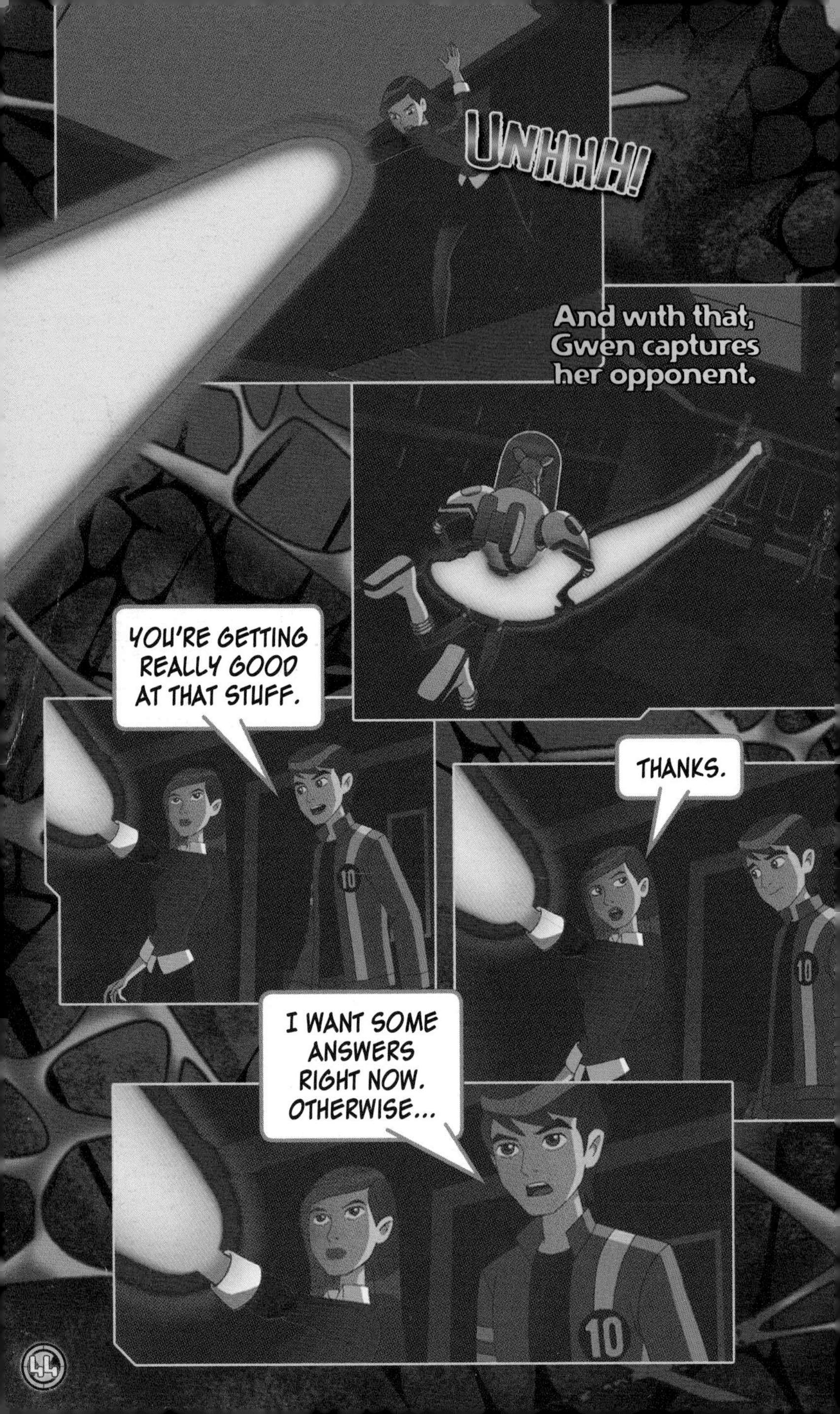
UNHHH!
And with that, Gwen captures her opponent.
YOU'RE GETTING REALLY GOOD AT THAT STUFF.
THANKS.
I WANT SOME ANSWERS RIGHT NOW. OTHERWISE...

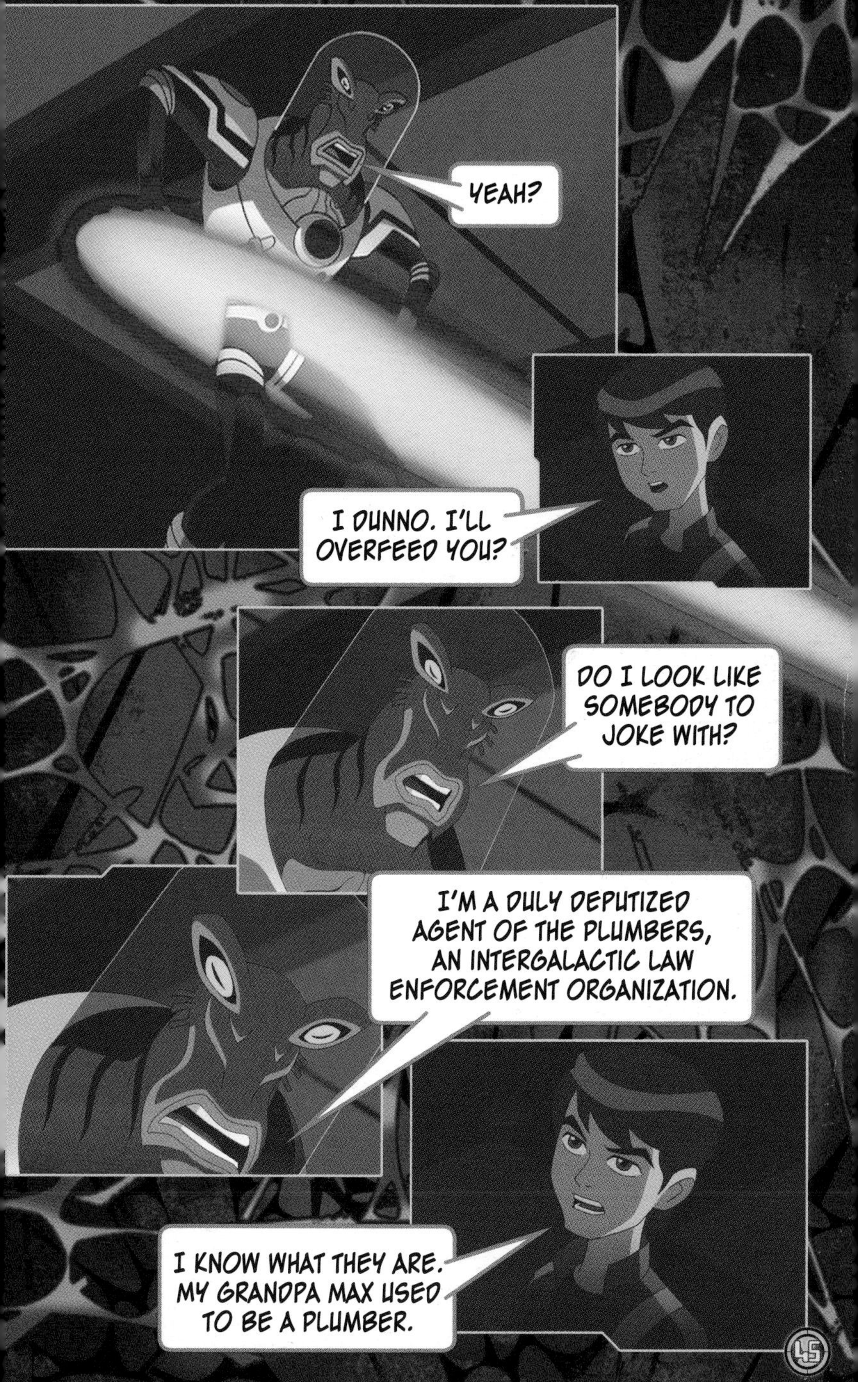
YEAH?
I DUNNO. I'LL OVERFEED YOU?
DO I LOOK LIKE SOMEBODY TO JOKE WITH?
I'M A DULY DEPUTIZED AGENT OF THE PLUMBERS, AN INTERGALACTIC LAW ENFORCEMENT ORGANIZATION.
I KNOW WHAT THEY ARE. MY GRANDPA MAX USED TO BE A PLUMBER.

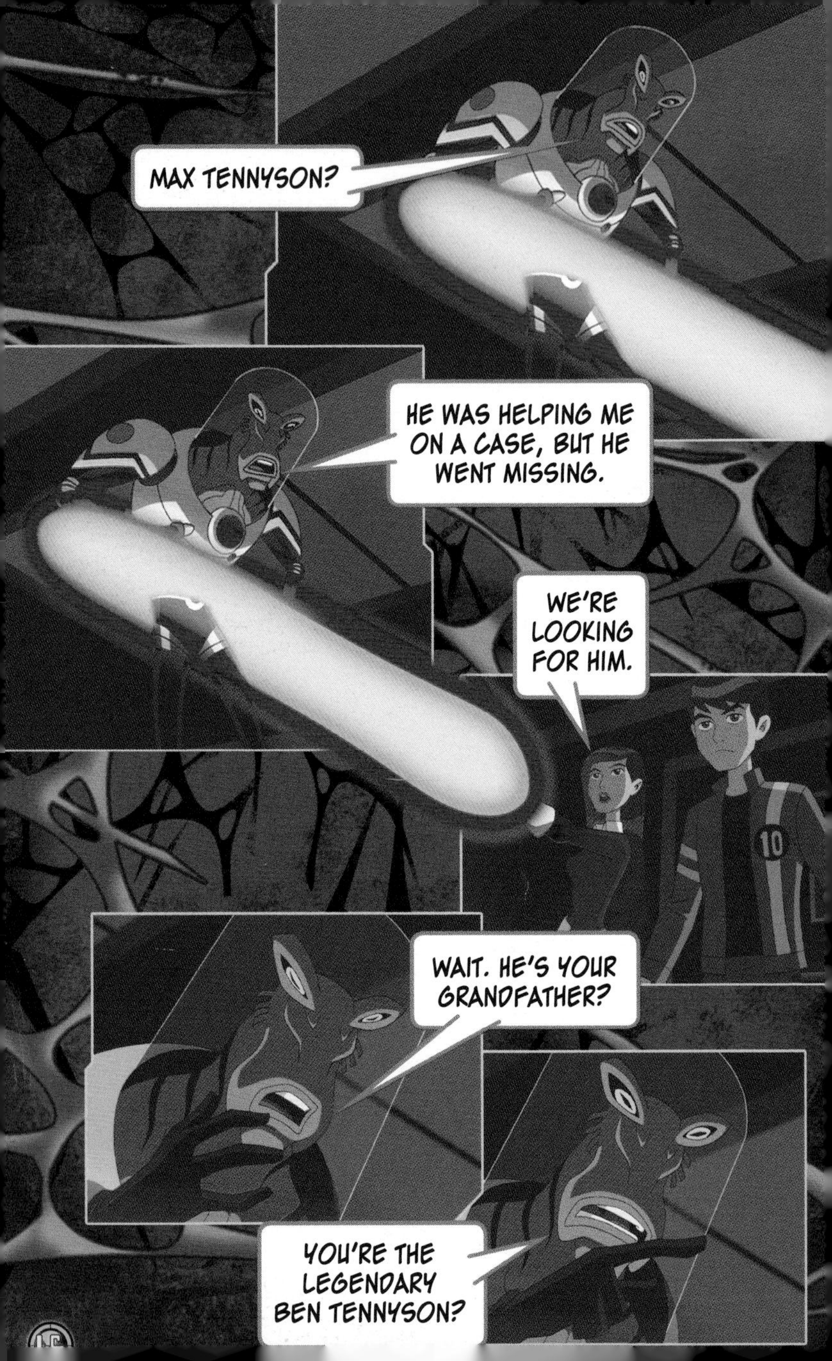
MAX TENNYSON?
HE WAS HELPING ME ON A CASE, BUT HE WENT MISSING.
WE'RE LOOKING FOR HIM.
WAIT. HE'S YOUR GRANDFATHER?
YOU'RE THE LEGENDARY BEN TENNYSON?

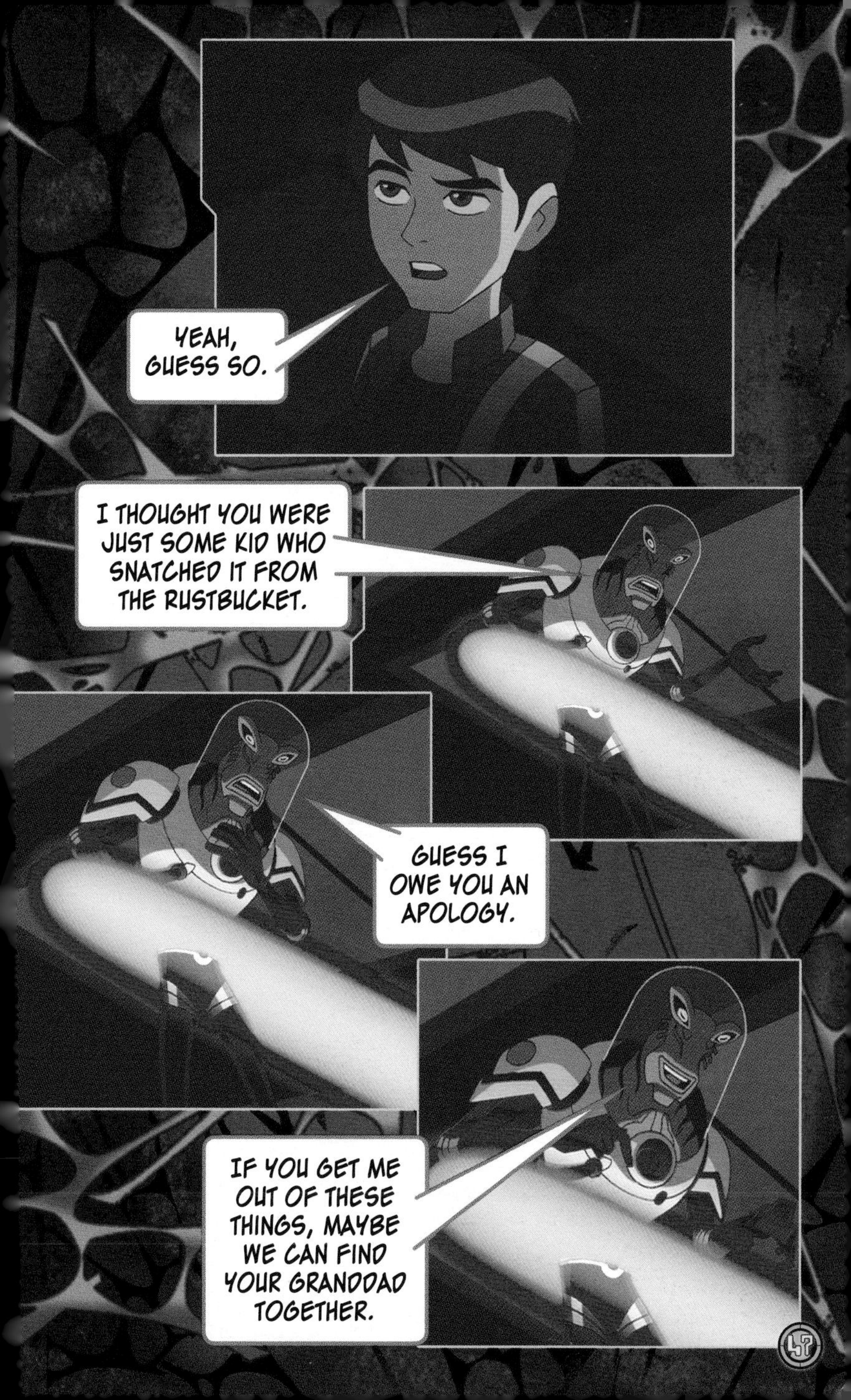
YEAH, GUESS SO.
I THOUGHT YOU WERE JUST SOME KID WHO SNATCHED IT FROM THE RUSTBUCKET.
GUESS I OWE YOU AN APOLOGY.
IF YOU GET ME OUT OF THESE THINGS, MAYBE WE CAN FIND YOUR GRANDDAD TOGETHER.

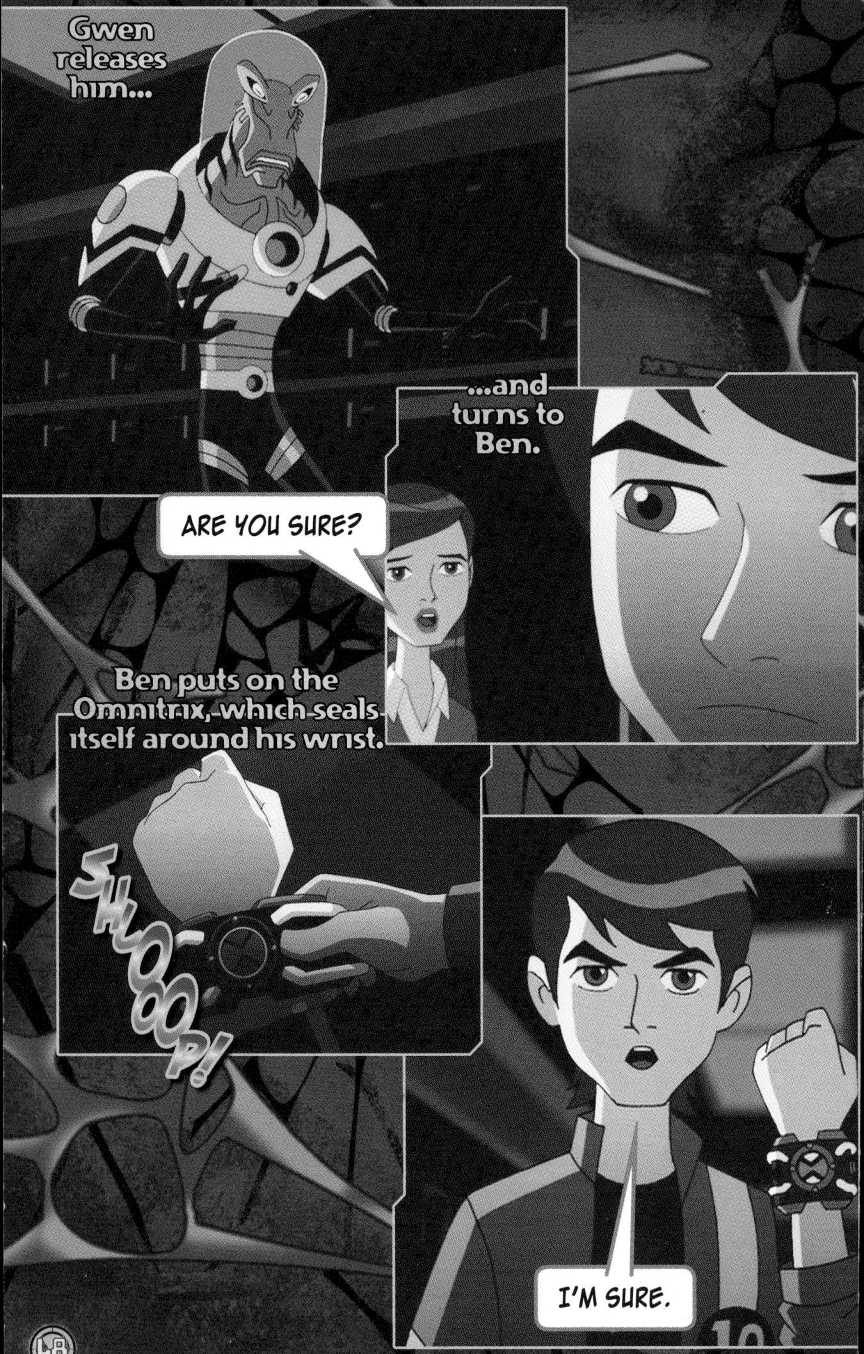
Gwen releases him...
...and turns to Ben.
ARE YOU SURE?
Ben puts on the Omnitrix, which seals itself around his wrist.
SHLOOOP!
I'M SURE.

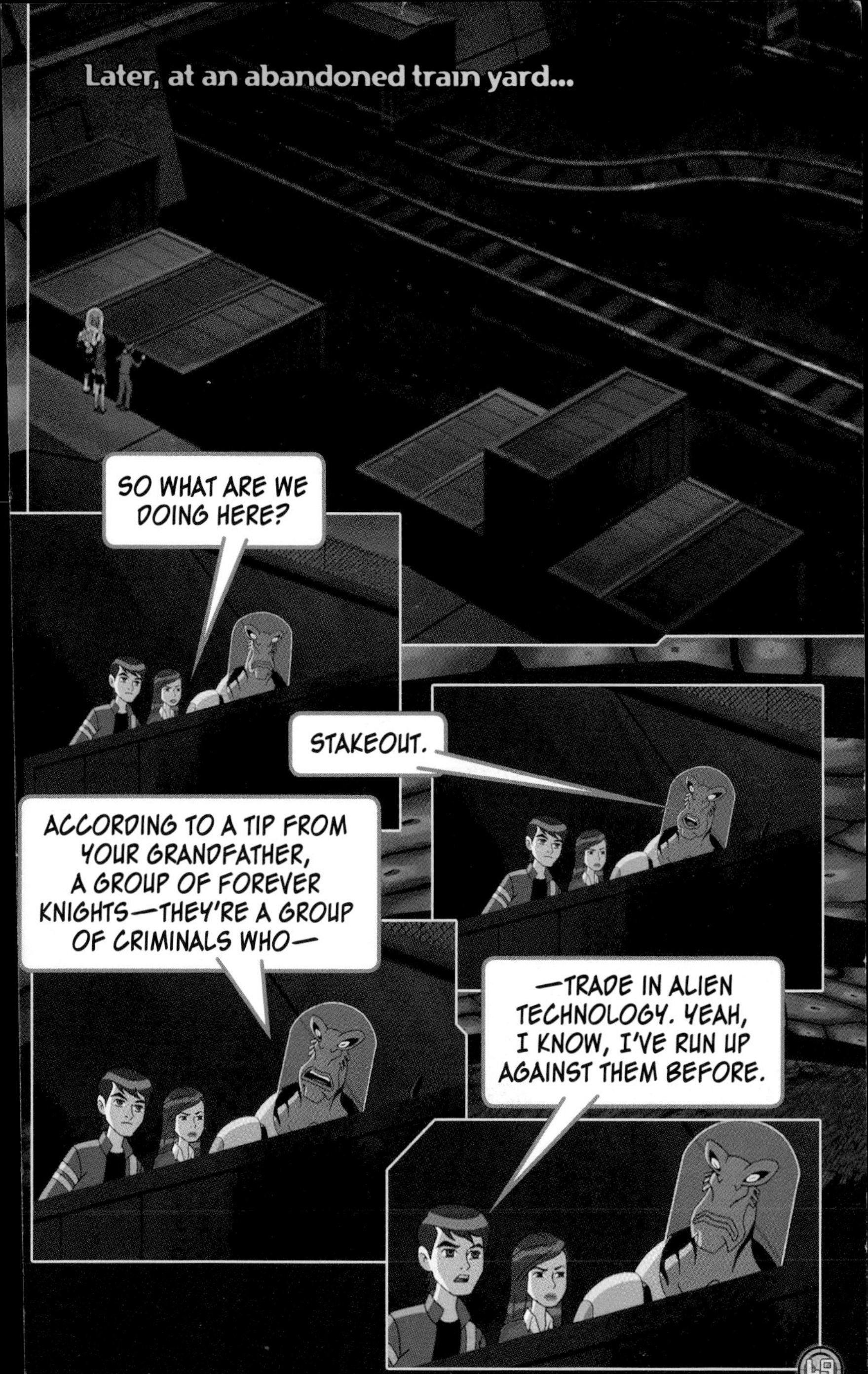
Later, at an abandoned train yard...
SO WHAT ARE WE DOING HERE?
STAKEOUT.
ACCORDING TO A TIP FROM YOUR GRANDFATHER, A GROUP OF FOREVER KNIGHTS—THEY'RE A GROUP OF CRIMINALS WHO—
—TRADE IN ALIEN TECHNOLOGY. YEAH, I KNOW, I'VE RUN UP AGAINST THEM BEFORE.

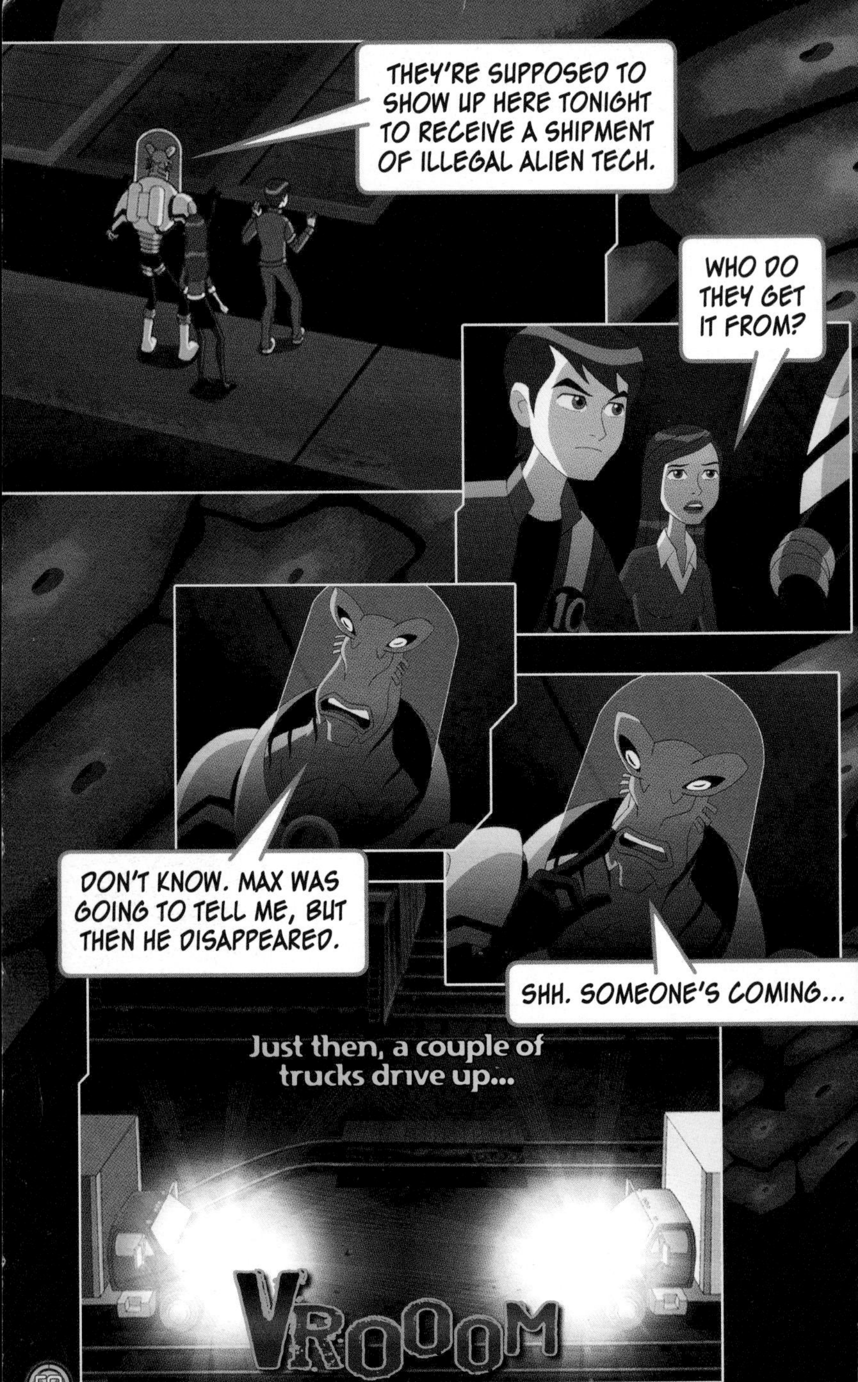
THEY'RE SUPPOSED TO SHOW UP HERE TONIGHT TO RECEIVE A SHIPMENT OF ILLEGAL ALIEN TECH.
WHO DO THEY GET IT FROM?
DON'T KNOW. MAX WAS GOING TO TELL ME, BUT THEN HE DISAPPEARED.
SHH. SOMEONE'S COMING...
Just then, a couple of trucks drive up...
VROOOM

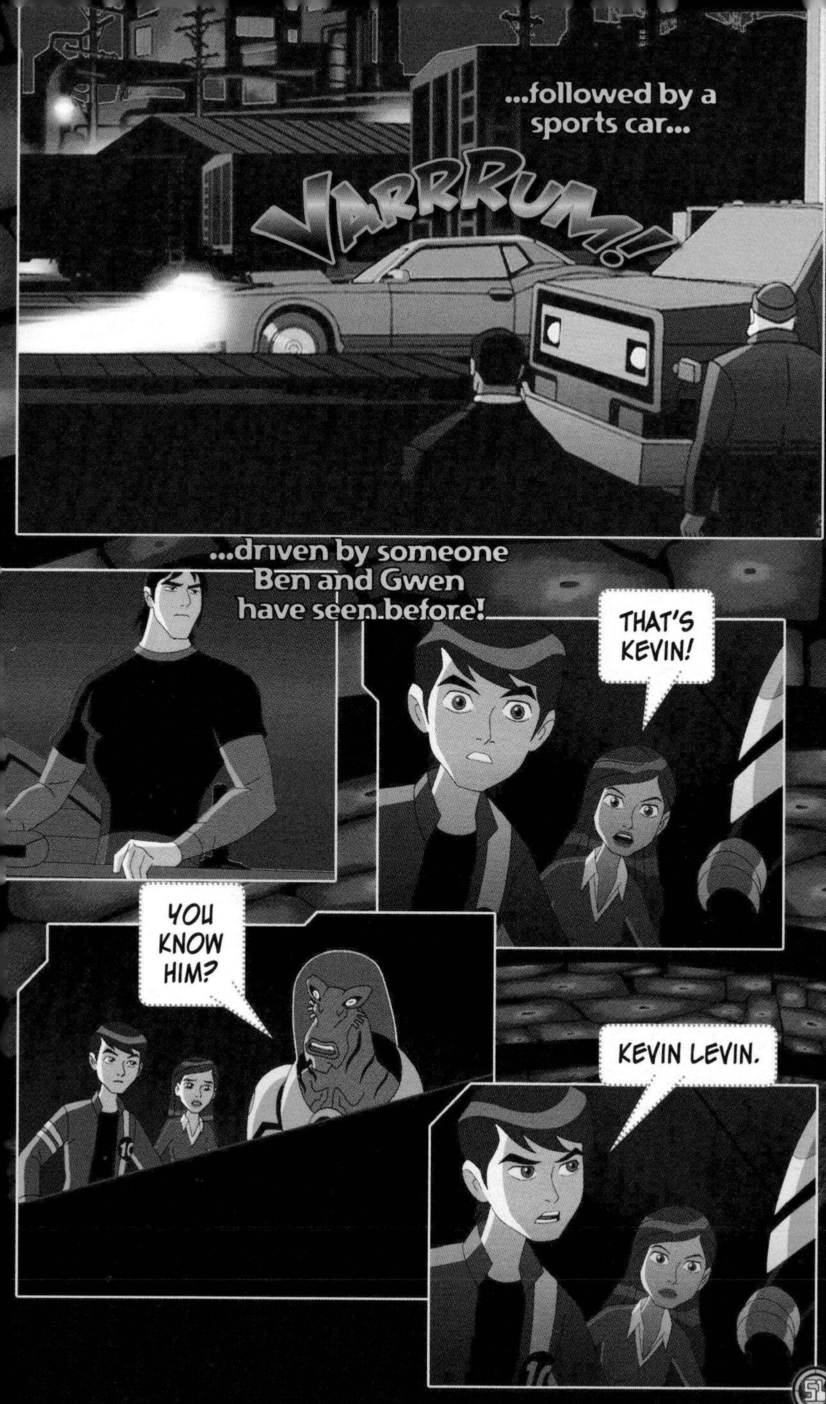
...followed by a sports car...
VARRRUM!!
...driven by someone Ben and Gwen have seen before!
THAT'S KEVIN!
YOU KNOW HIM?
KEVIN LEVIN.

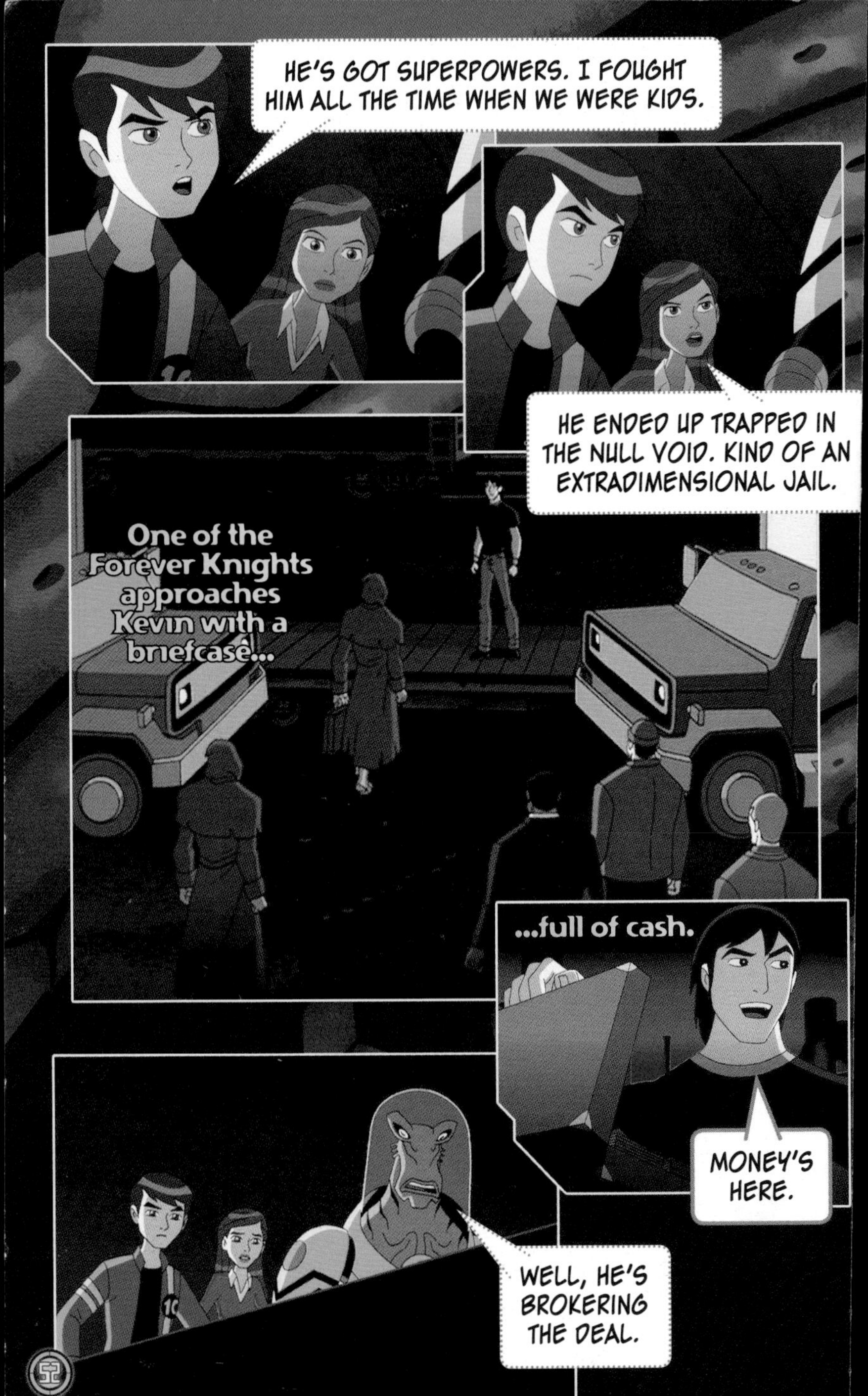
HE'S GOT SUPERPOWERS. I FOUGHT HIM ALL THE TIME WHEN WE WERE KIDS.
HE ENDED UP TRAPPED IN THE NULL VOID. KIND OF AN EXTRADIMENSIONAL JAIL.
One of the Forever Knights approaches Kevin with a briefcase...
...full of cash.
MONEY'S HERE.
WELL, HE'S BROKERING THE DEAL.

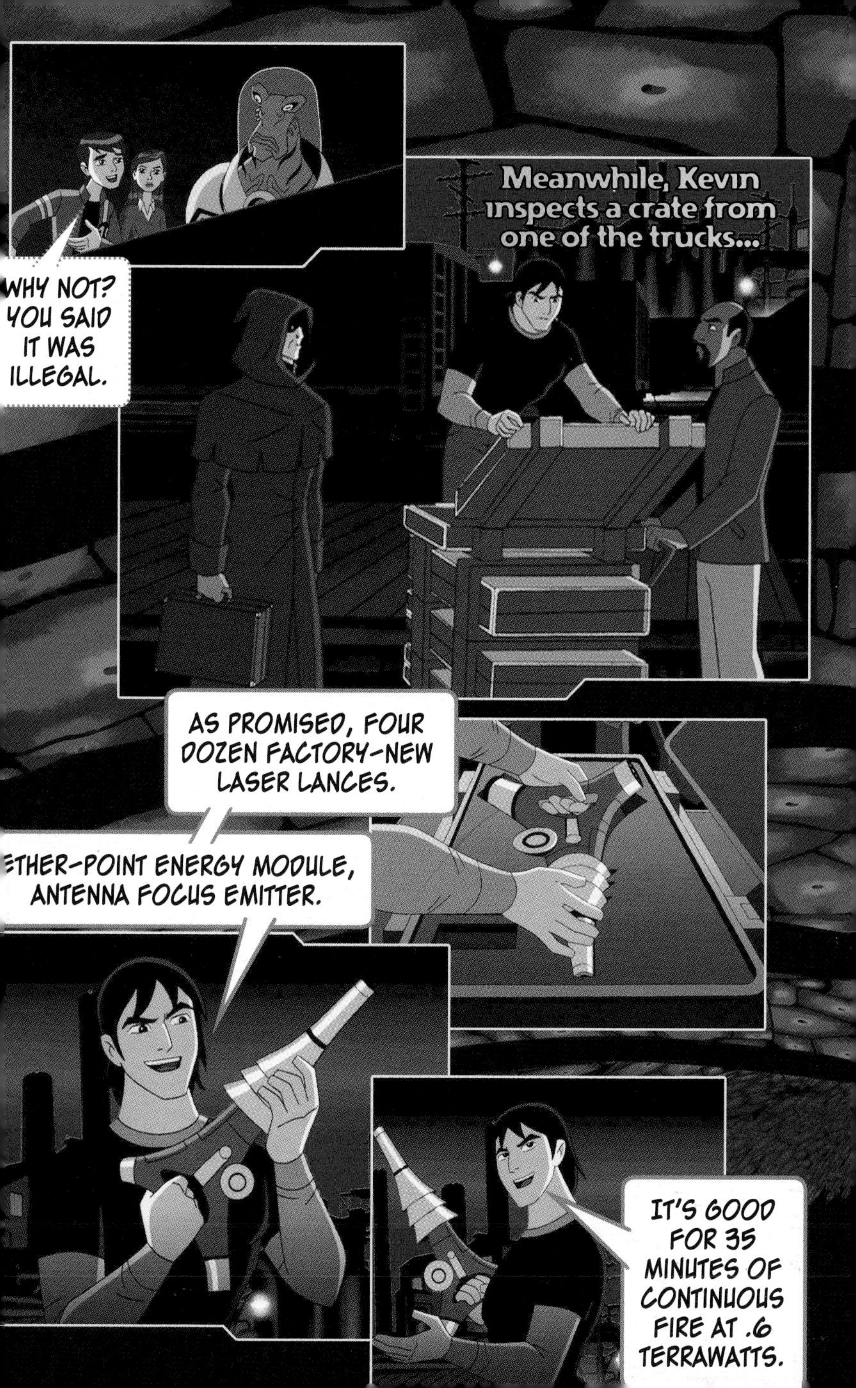
WHY NOT? YOU SAID IT WAS ILLEGAL.
Meanwhile, Kevin inspects a crate from one of the trucks...
AS PROMISED, FOUR DOZEN FACTORY-NEW LASER LANCES.
ETHER-POINT ENERGY MODULE, ANTENNA FOCUS EMITTER.
IT'S GOOD FOR 35 MINUTES OF CONTINUOUS FIRE AT .6 TERRAWATTS.

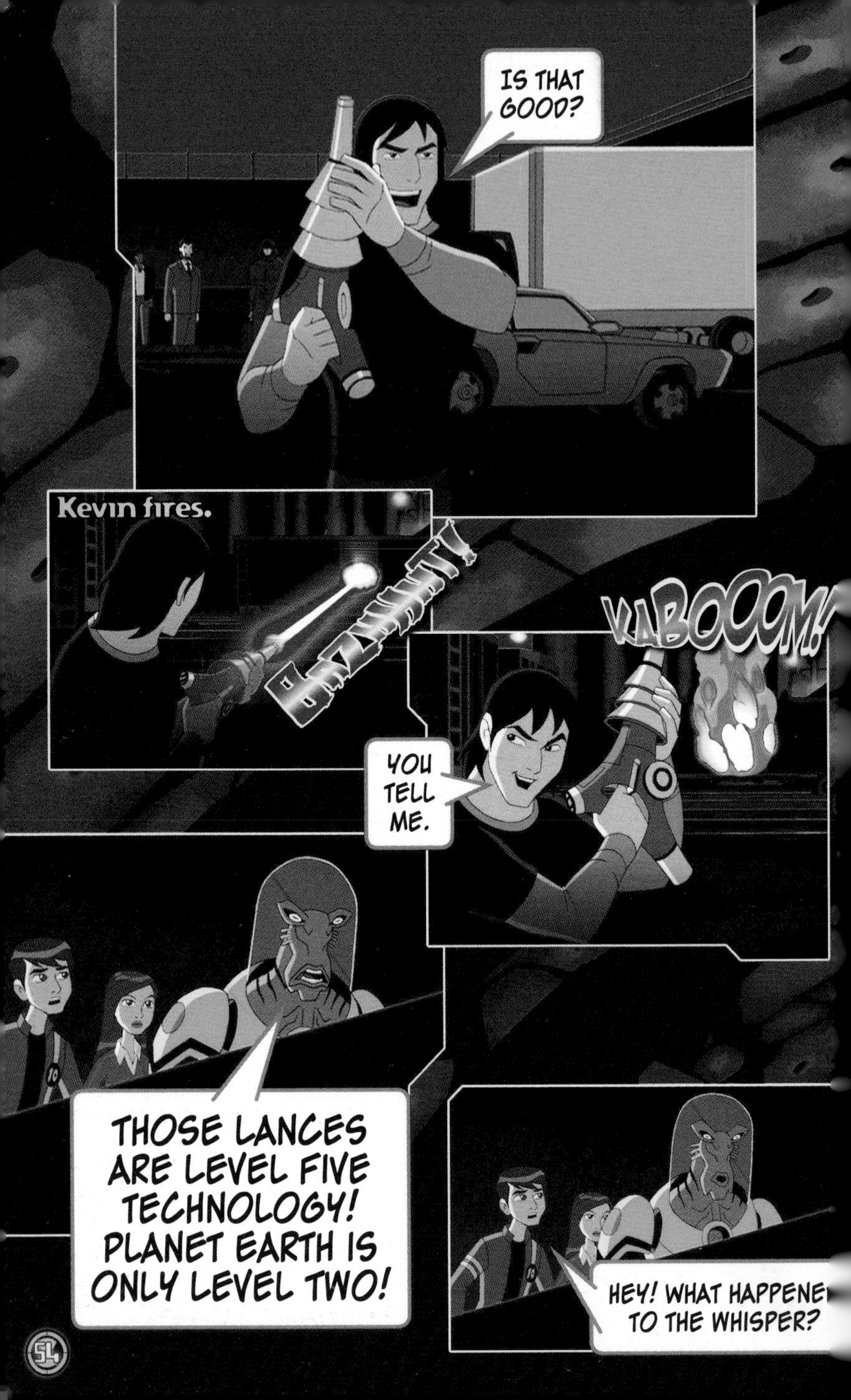
IS THAT GOOD?
Kevin fires.
KABOOOM!
YOU TELL ME.
THOSE LANCES ARE LEVEL FIVE TECHNOLOGY! PLANET EARTH IS ONLY LEVEL TWO!
HEY! WHAT HAPPENE TO THE WHISPER?

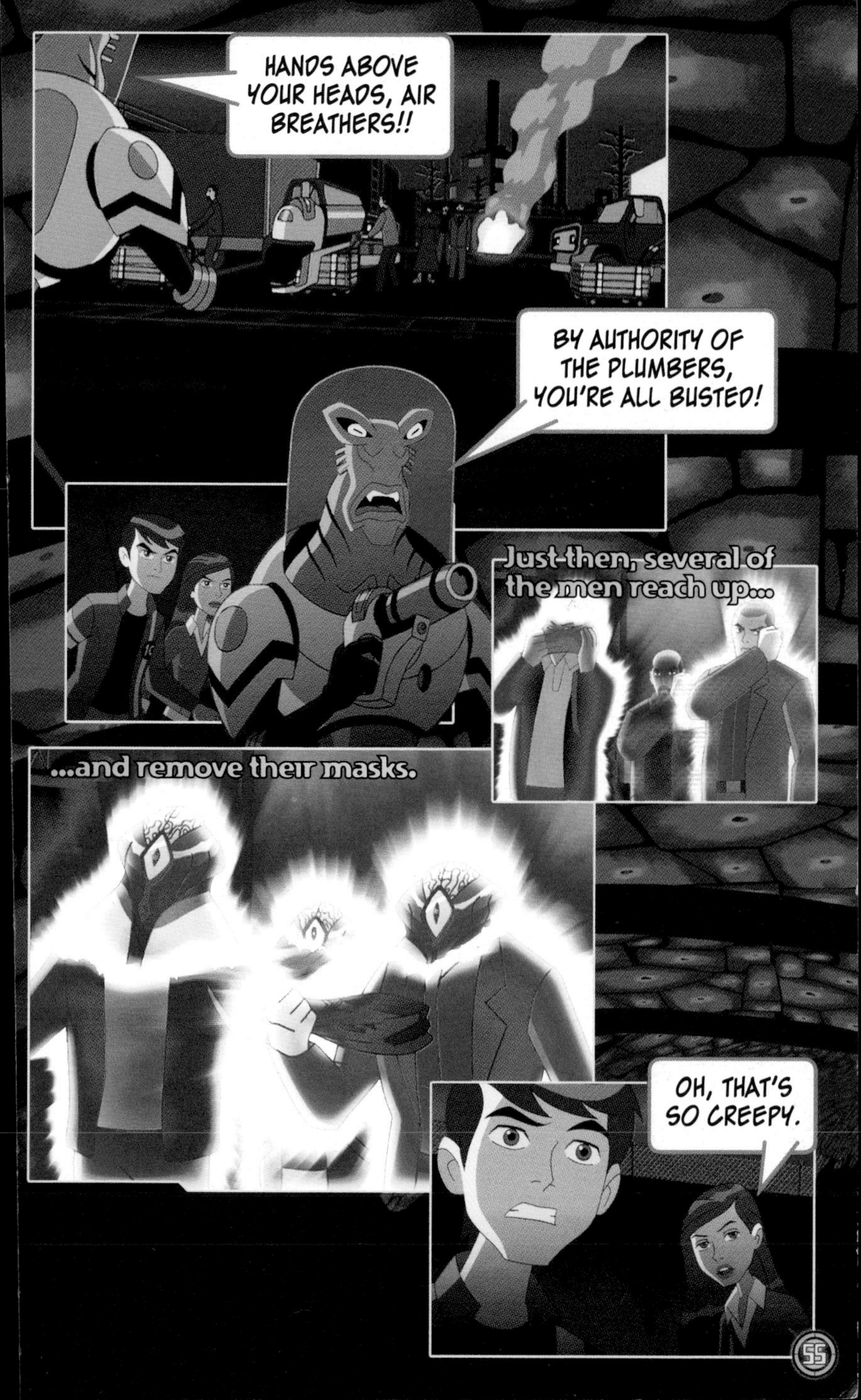
HANDS ABOVE YOUR HEADS, AIR BREATHERS!!
BY AUTHORITY OF THE PLUMBERS, YOU'RE ALL BUSTED!
Just then, several of the men reach up...
...and remove their masks.
OH, THAT'S SO CREEPY.
55

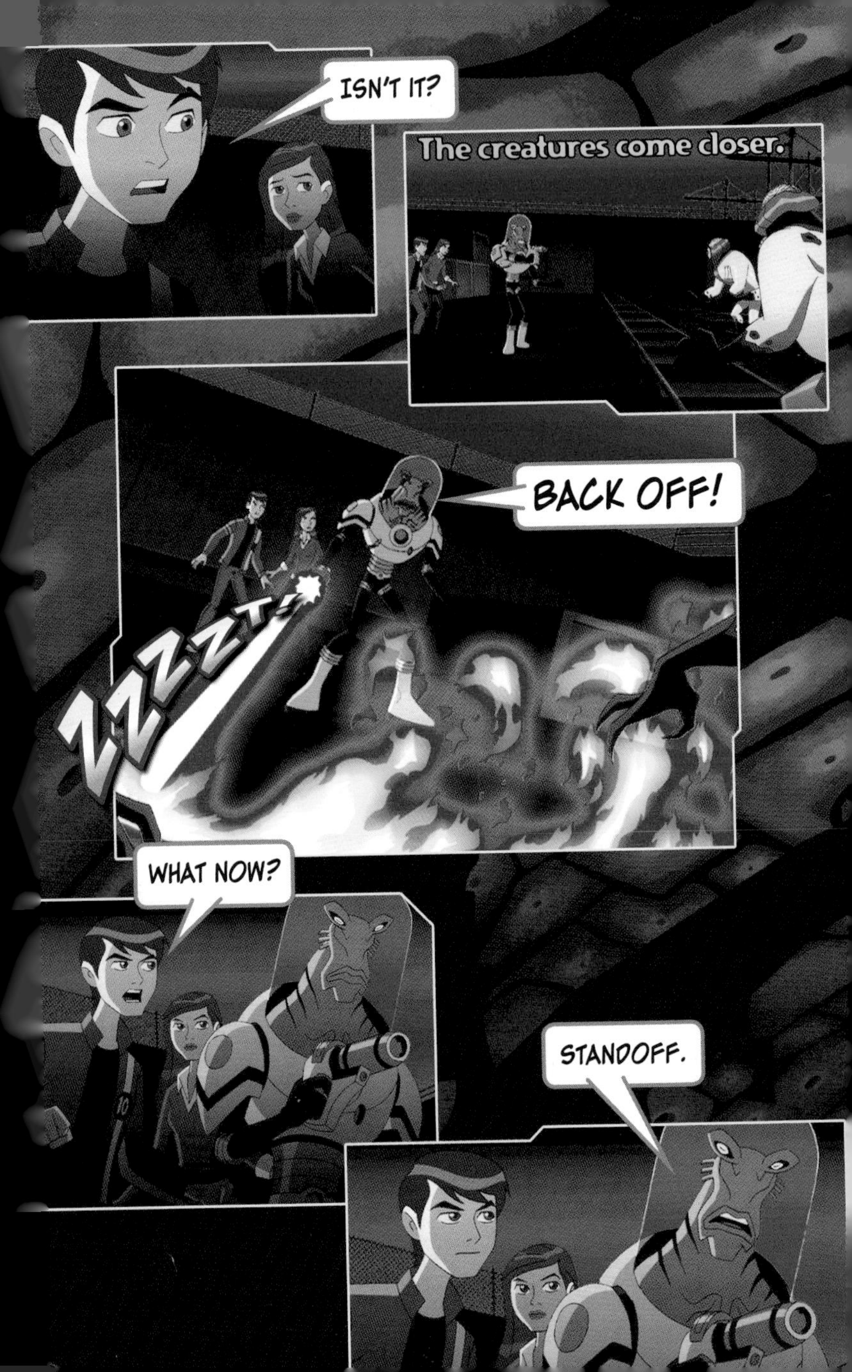
ISN'T IT?
The creatures come closer.
BACK OFF!
ZZZZZT!
WHAT NOW?
STANDOFF.

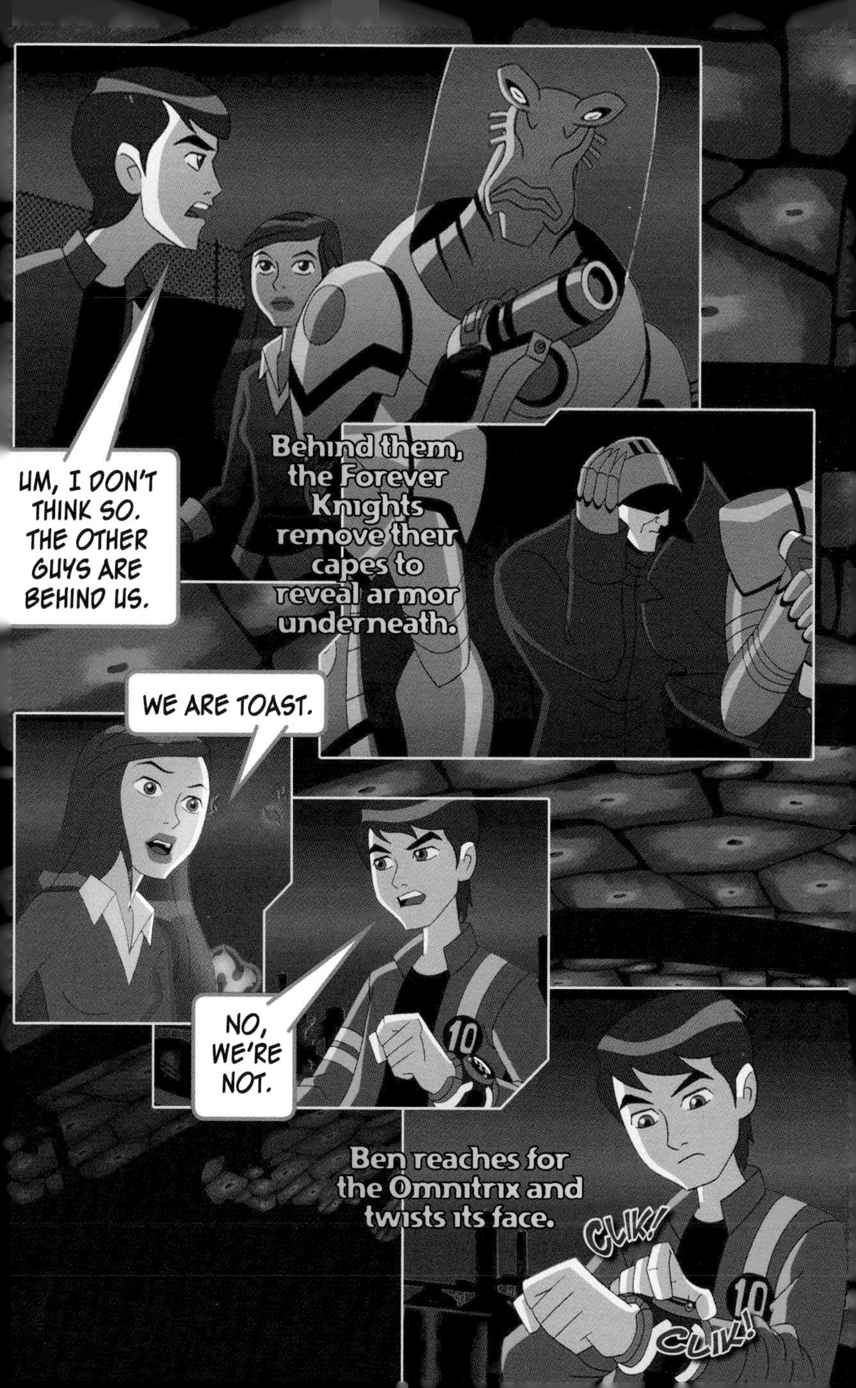
UM, I DON'T THINK SO. THE OTHER GUYS ARE BEHIND US.
Behind them, the Forever Knights remove their capes to reveal armor underneath.
WE ARE TOAST.
NO, WE'RE NOT.
Ben reaches for the Omnitrix and twists its face.
CLIK!
CLIK!

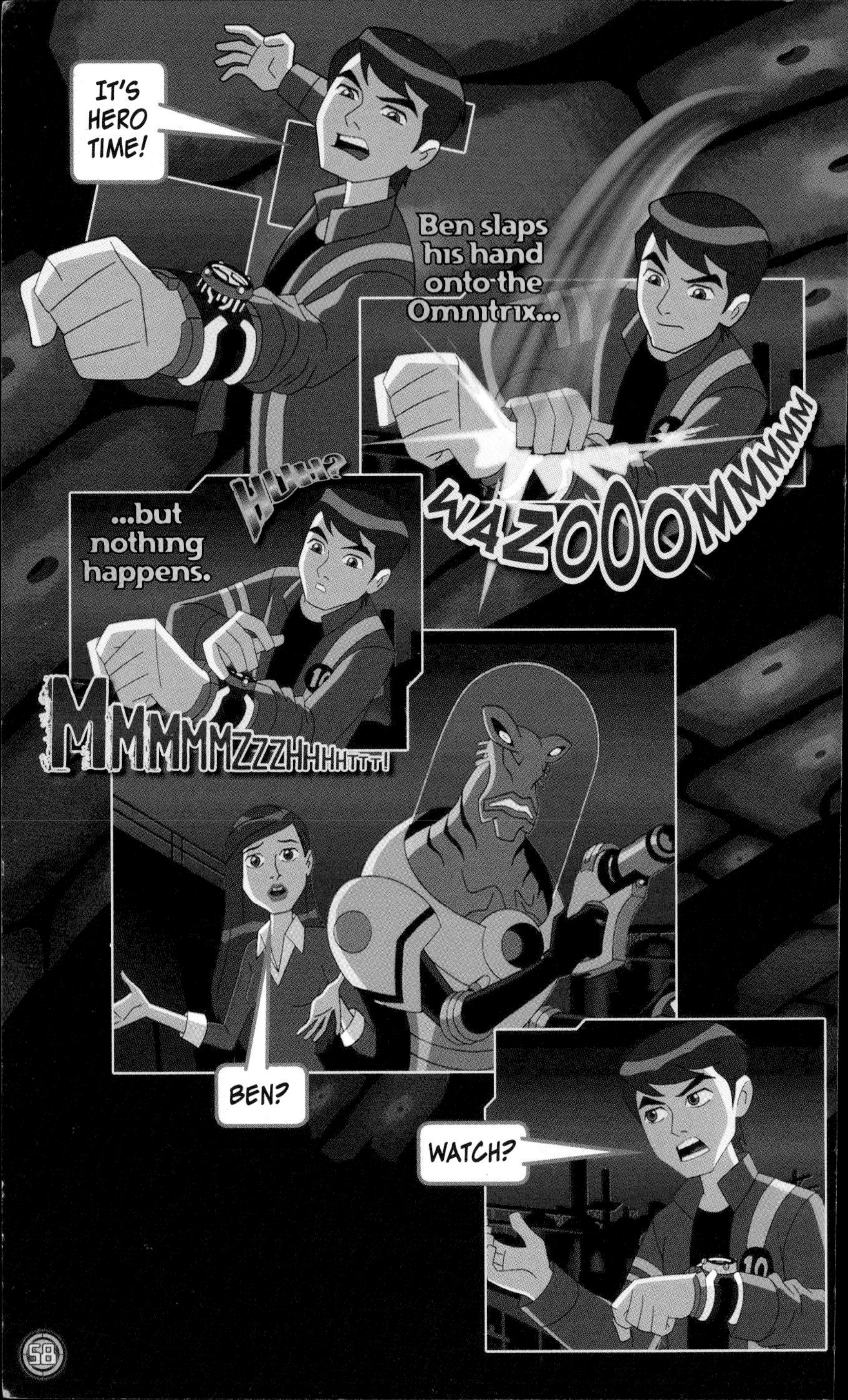
IT'S HERO TIME!
Ben slaps his hand onto the Omnitrix...
WAZOOOMMMMM
HUHH?
...but nothing happens.
MMMMMZZZHHHTTT!
BEN?
WATCH?

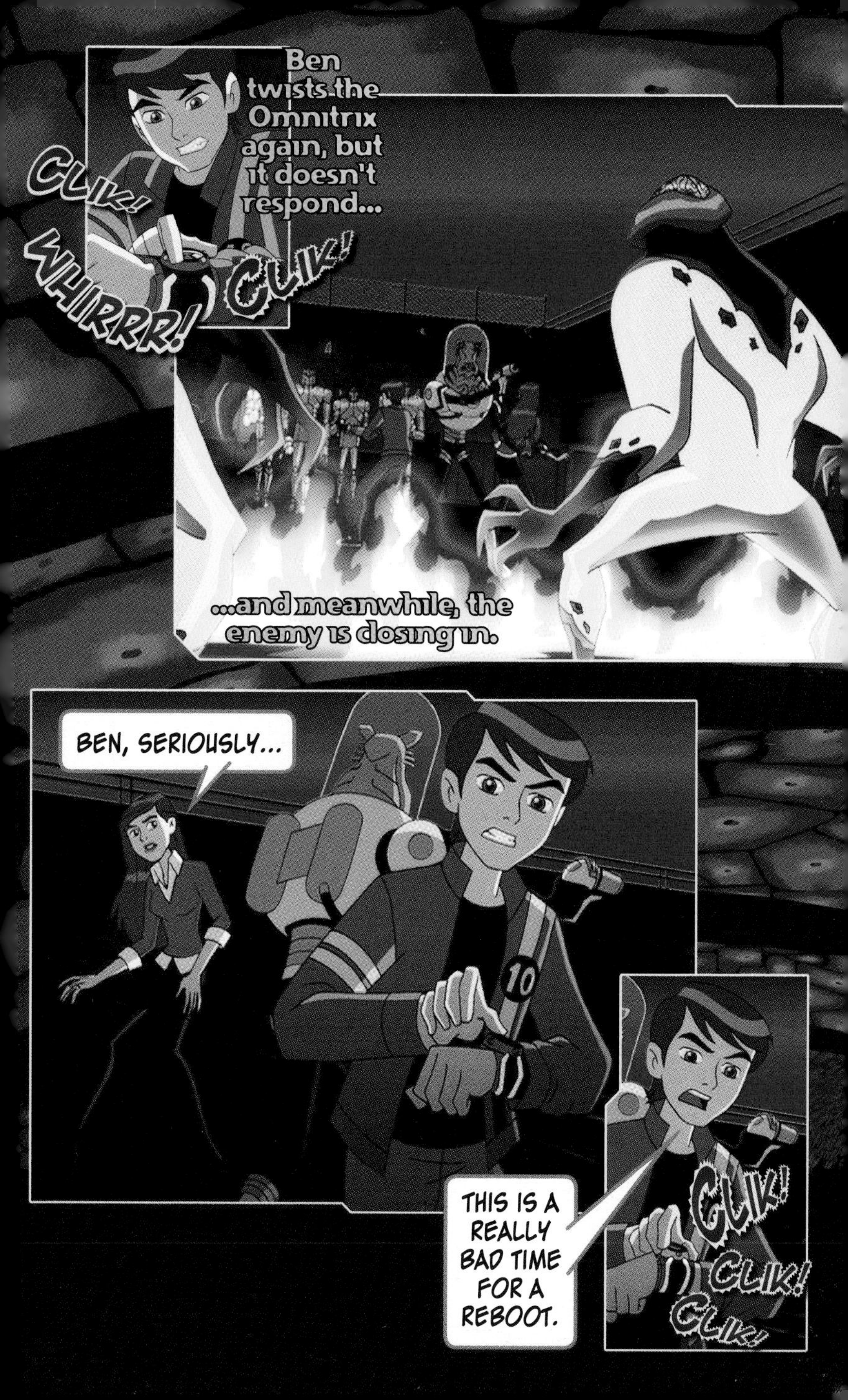
Ben twists the Omnitrix again, but it doesn't respond...
CLIK!
WHIRRR!
CLIK!
...and meanwhile, the enemy is closing in.
BEN, SERIOUSLY...
THIS IS A REALLY BAD TIME FOR A REBOOT.
CLIK!
CLIK!
CLIK!

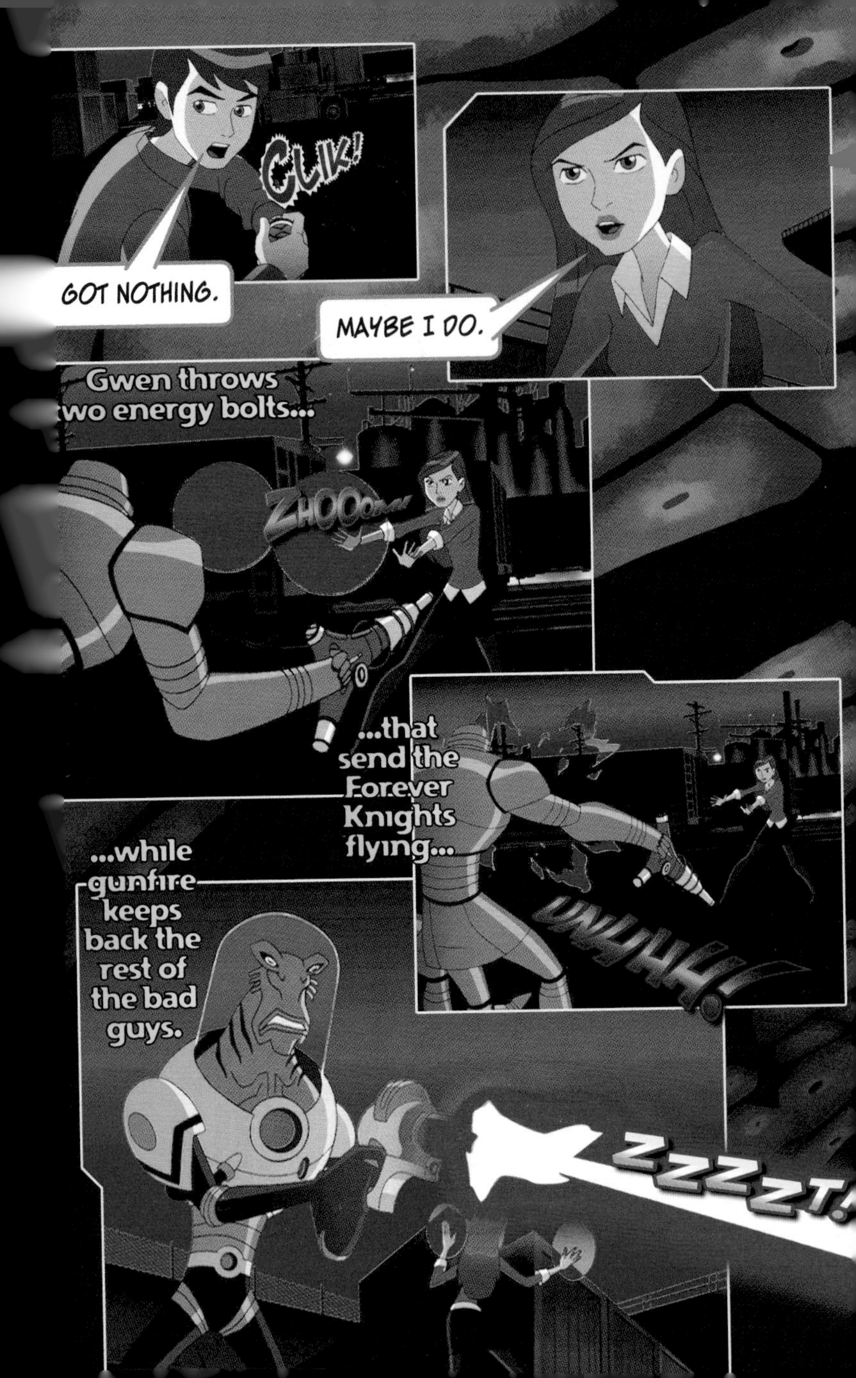
CLIK!
GOT NOTHING.
MAYBE I DO.
Gwen throws two energy bolts...
ZHOOOM
...that send the Forever Knights flying...
UNHH!
...while gunfire keeps back the rest of the bad guys.
ZZZZT!

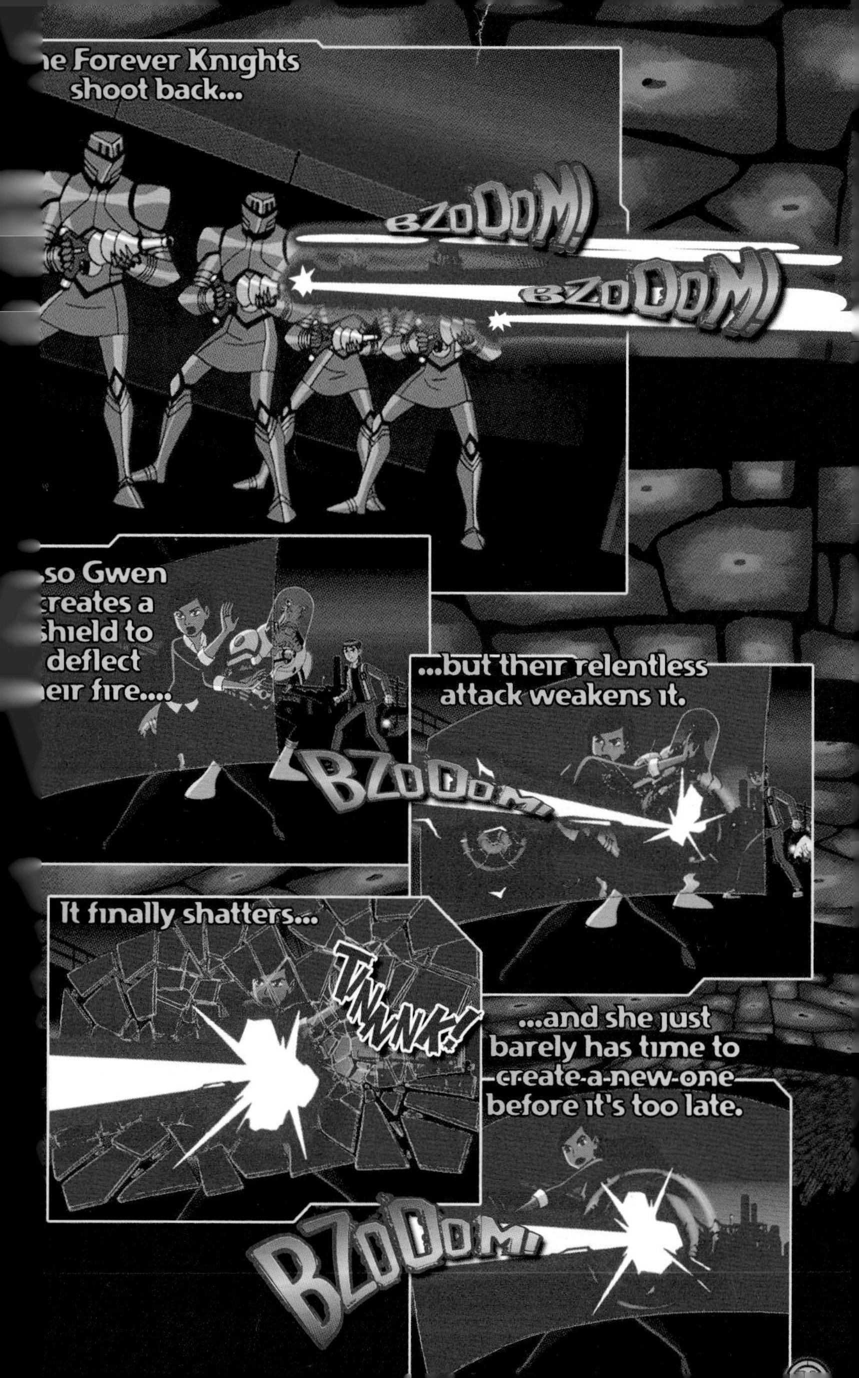

he Forever Knights shoot back...
BZOOOM!
BZOOOM!
so Gwen creates a shield to deflect heir fire....
BZOOOM!
...but their relentless attack weakens it.
It finally shatters...
TINNNK!
...and she just barely has time to create a new one before it's too late.
BZOOOM!

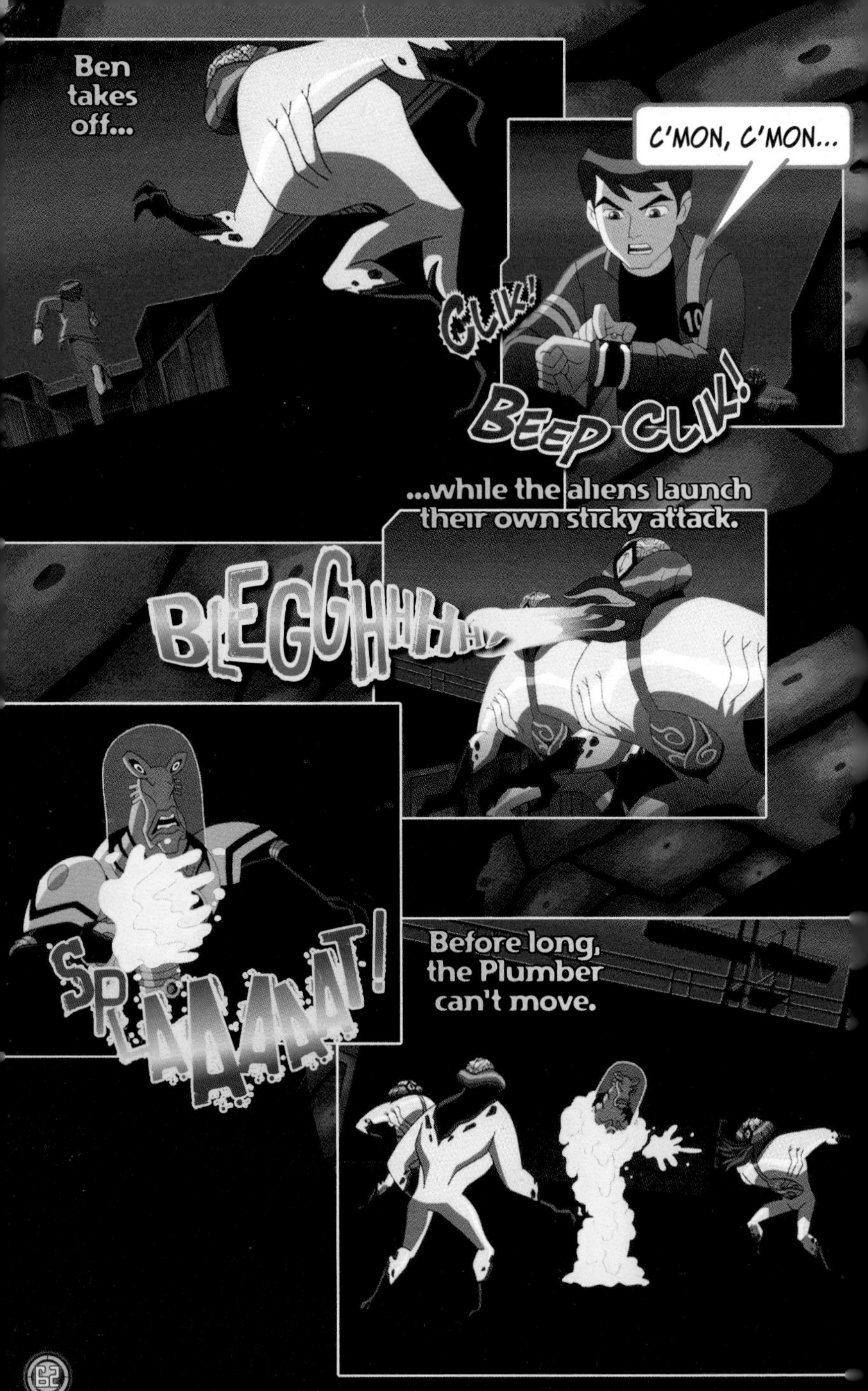
Ben takes off...
C'MON, C'MON...
CLIK!
BEEP CLIK!
...while the aliens launch their own sticky attack.
BLEGGHHHH
SPLAAAAAT!
Before long, the Plumber can't move.

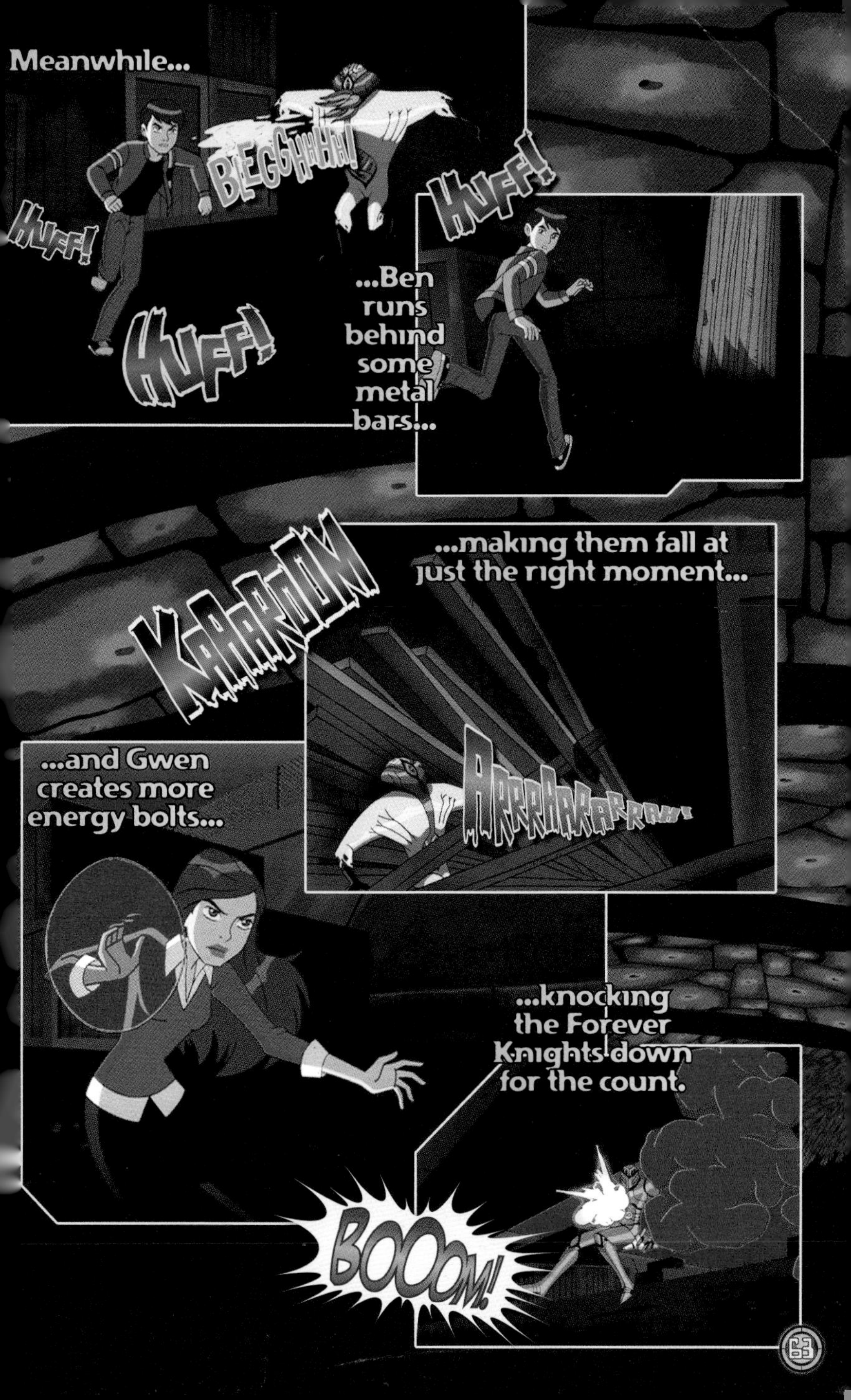
Meanwhile...
BLEGGHHHH!
HUFF!
HUFF!
...Ben runs behind some metal bars...
HUFF!
KAARROOM
...making them fall at just the right moment...
ARRRARARRRAH!
...and Gwen creates more energy bolts...
...knocking the Forever Knights down for the count.
BOOOM!

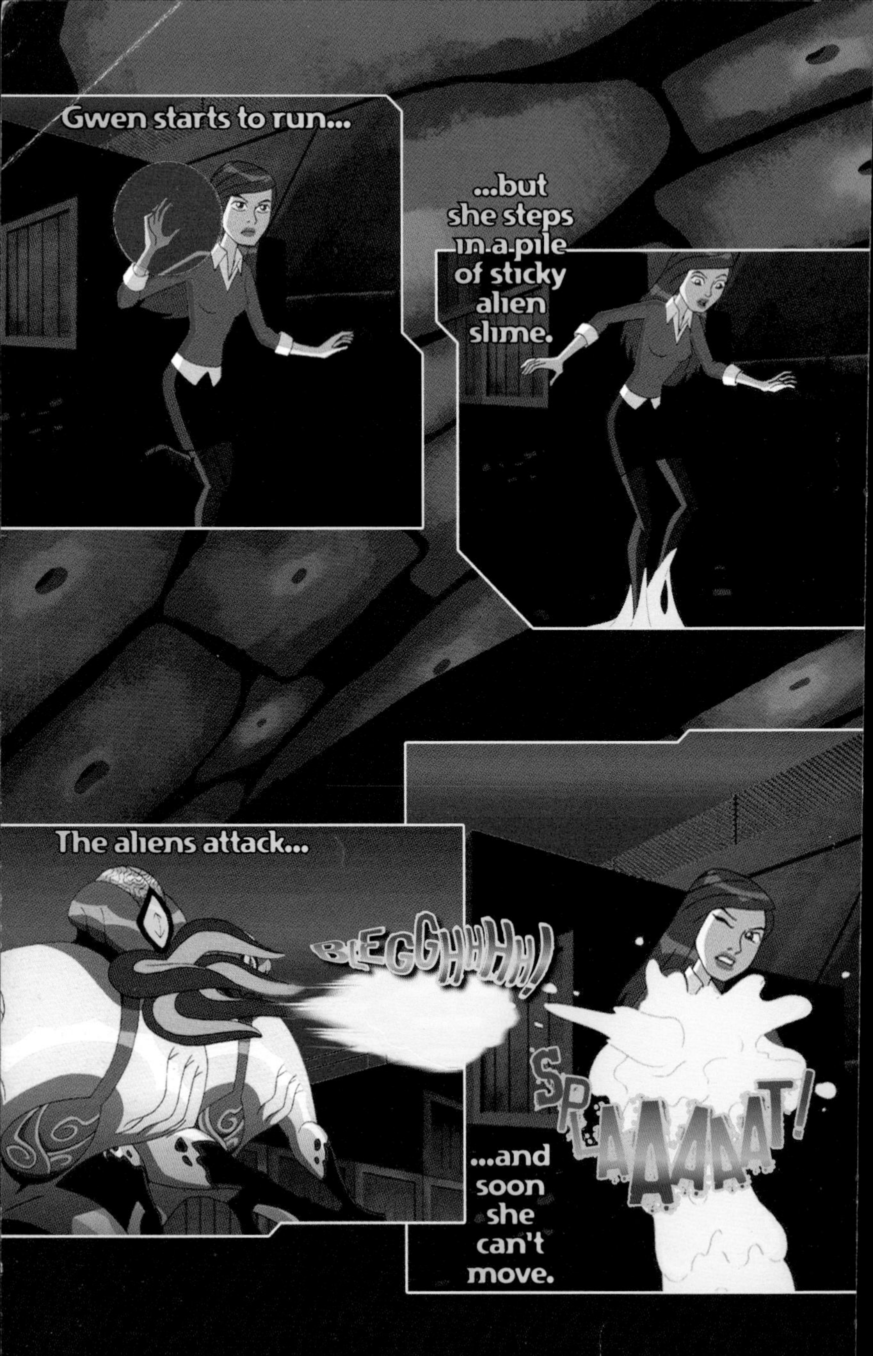
Gwen starts to run...
...but she steps in a pile of sticky alien slime.
The aliens attack...
BLEGGHHHH!
SPLAAAAAT!
...and soon she can't move.

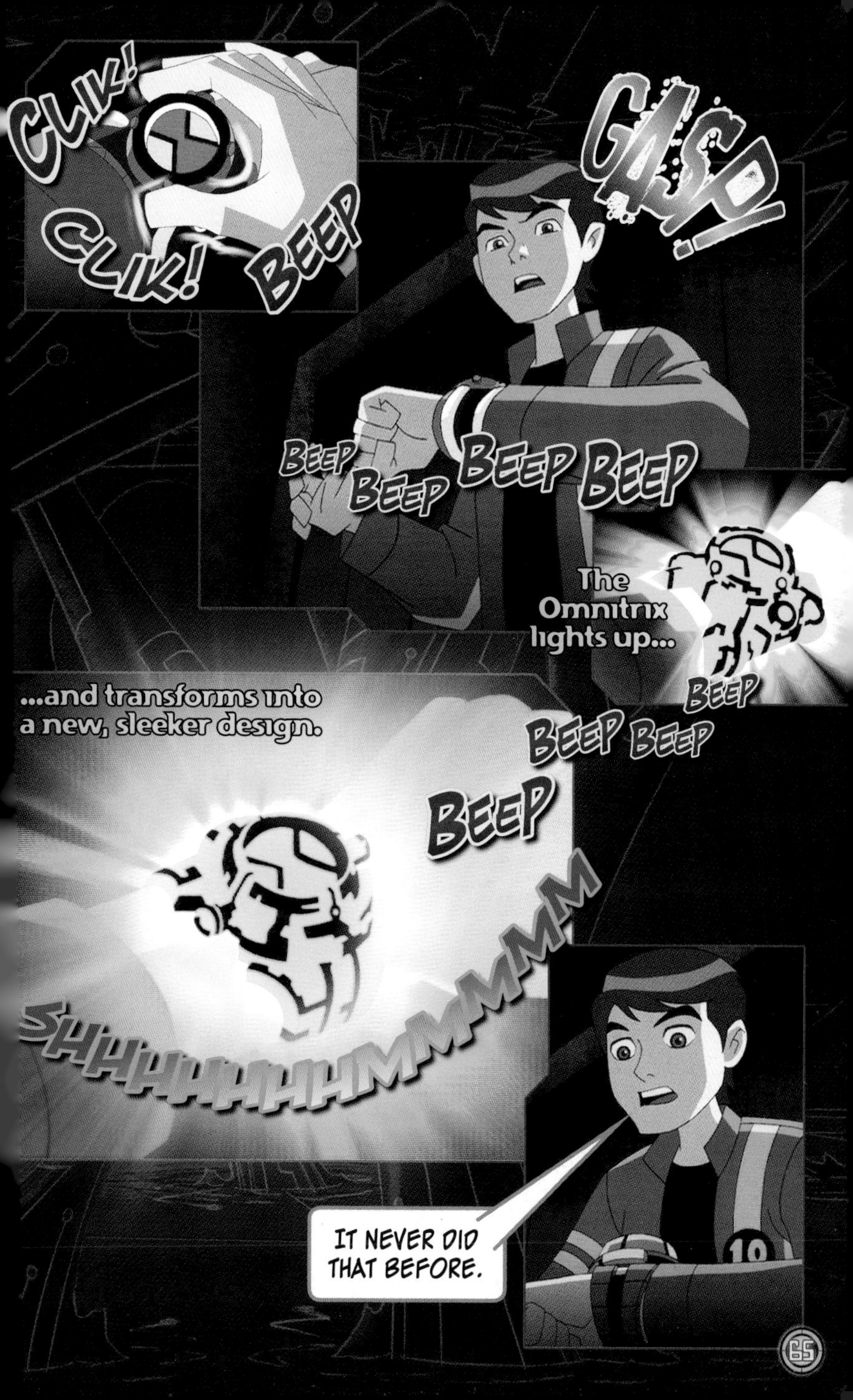

CLIK!
CLIK!
BEEP
GASP!
BEEP
BEEP
BEEP
BEEP
The Omnitrix lights up...
BEEP
...and transforms into a new, sleeker design.
BEEP BEEP
BEEP
SHHHHHHHMMMMMM
IT NEVER DID THAT BEFORE.

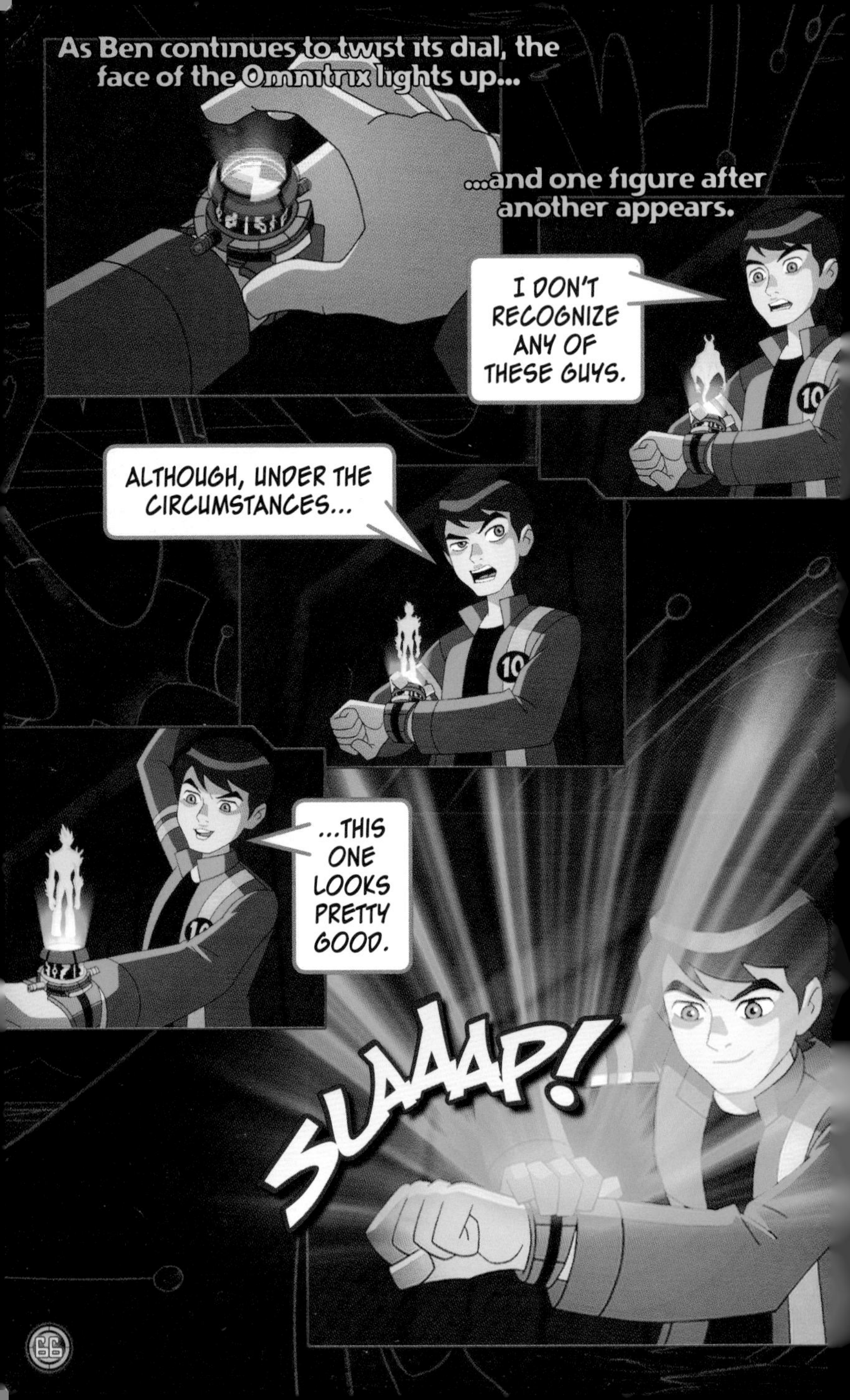

As Ben continues to twist its dial, the face of the Omnitrix lights up...
...and one figure after another appears.
I DON'T RECOGNIZE ANY OF THESE GUYS.
ALTHOUGH, UNDER THE CIRCUMSTANCES...
...THIS ONE LOOKS PRETTY GOOD.
SLAAAP!

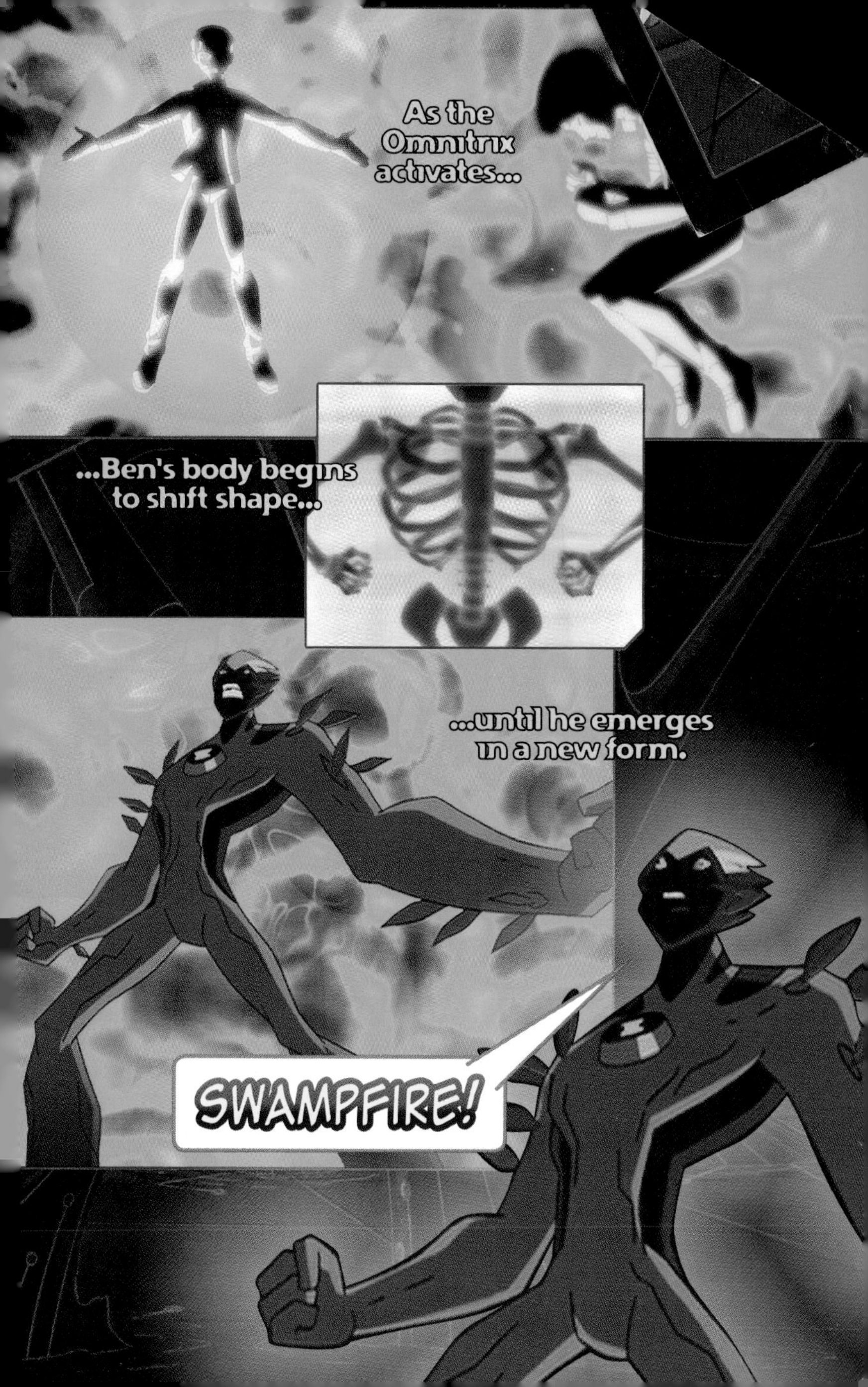
As the Omnitrix activates...
...Ben's body begins to shift shape...
...until he emerges in a new form.
SWAMPFIRE!

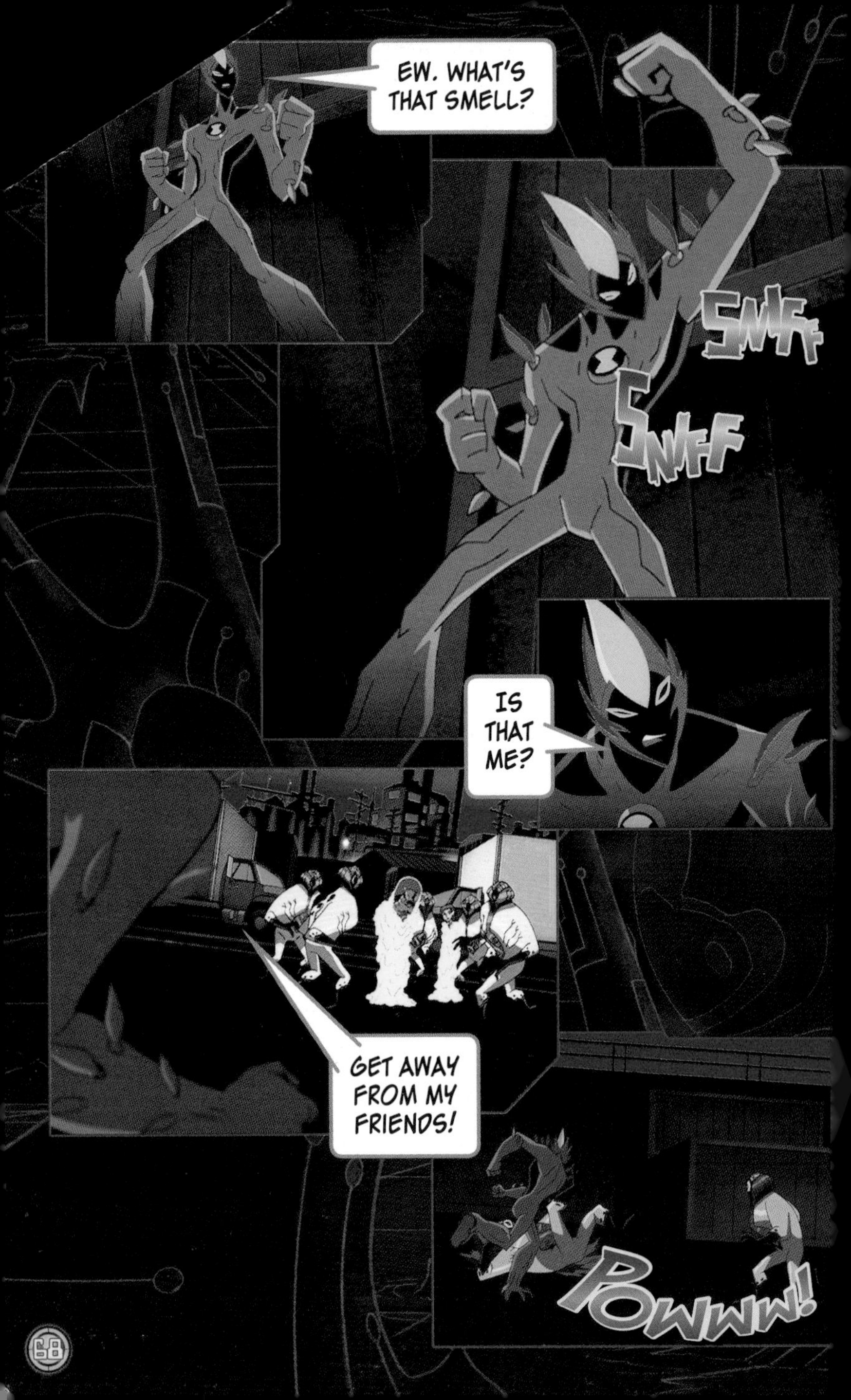
EW. WHAT'S THAT SMELL?
SNIFF
SNIFF
IS THAT ME?
GET AWAY FROM MY FRIENDS!
POWWW!

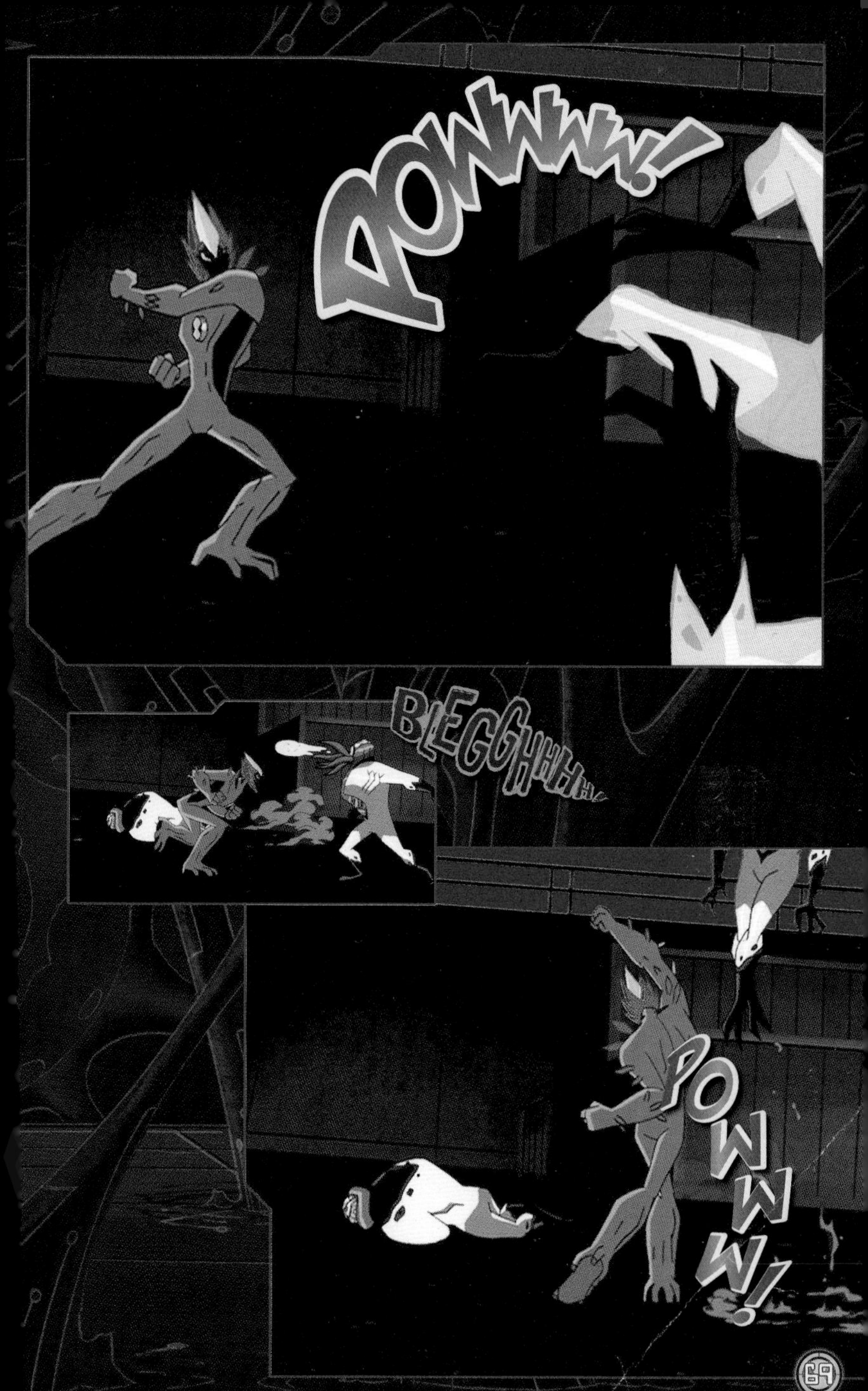
POWWWW!
BLEGGHHHH
POWWWW!

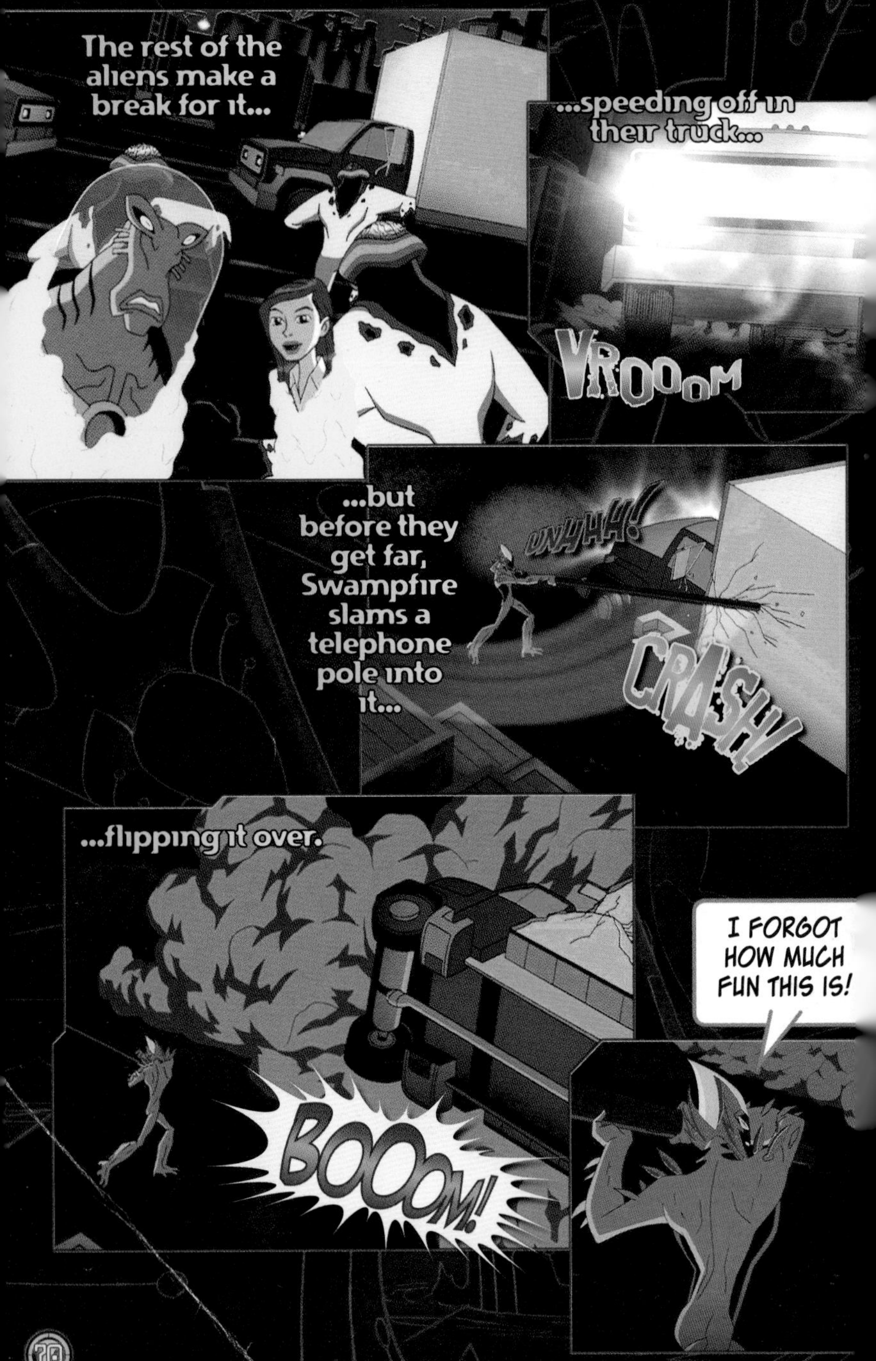
The rest of the aliens make a break for it...
...speeding off in their truck...
VROOOOM
...but before they get far, Swampfire slams a telephone pole into it...
UNHHH!
CRASH!
...flipping it over.
BOOOM!
I FORGOT HOW MUCH FUN THIS IS!

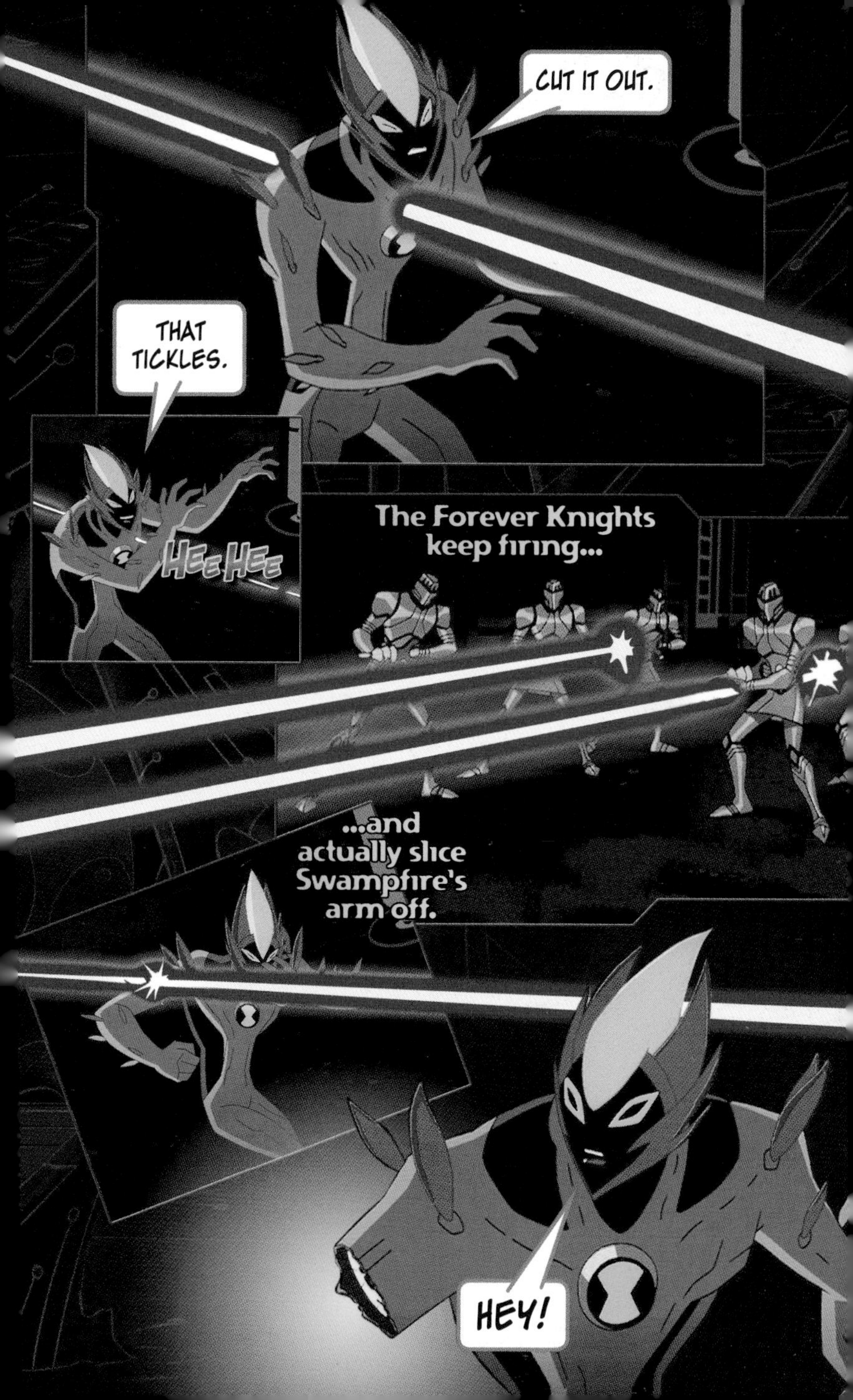
CUT IT OUT.
THAT TICKLES.
HEE HEE
The Forever Knights keep firing...
...and actually slice Swampfire's arm off.
HEY!

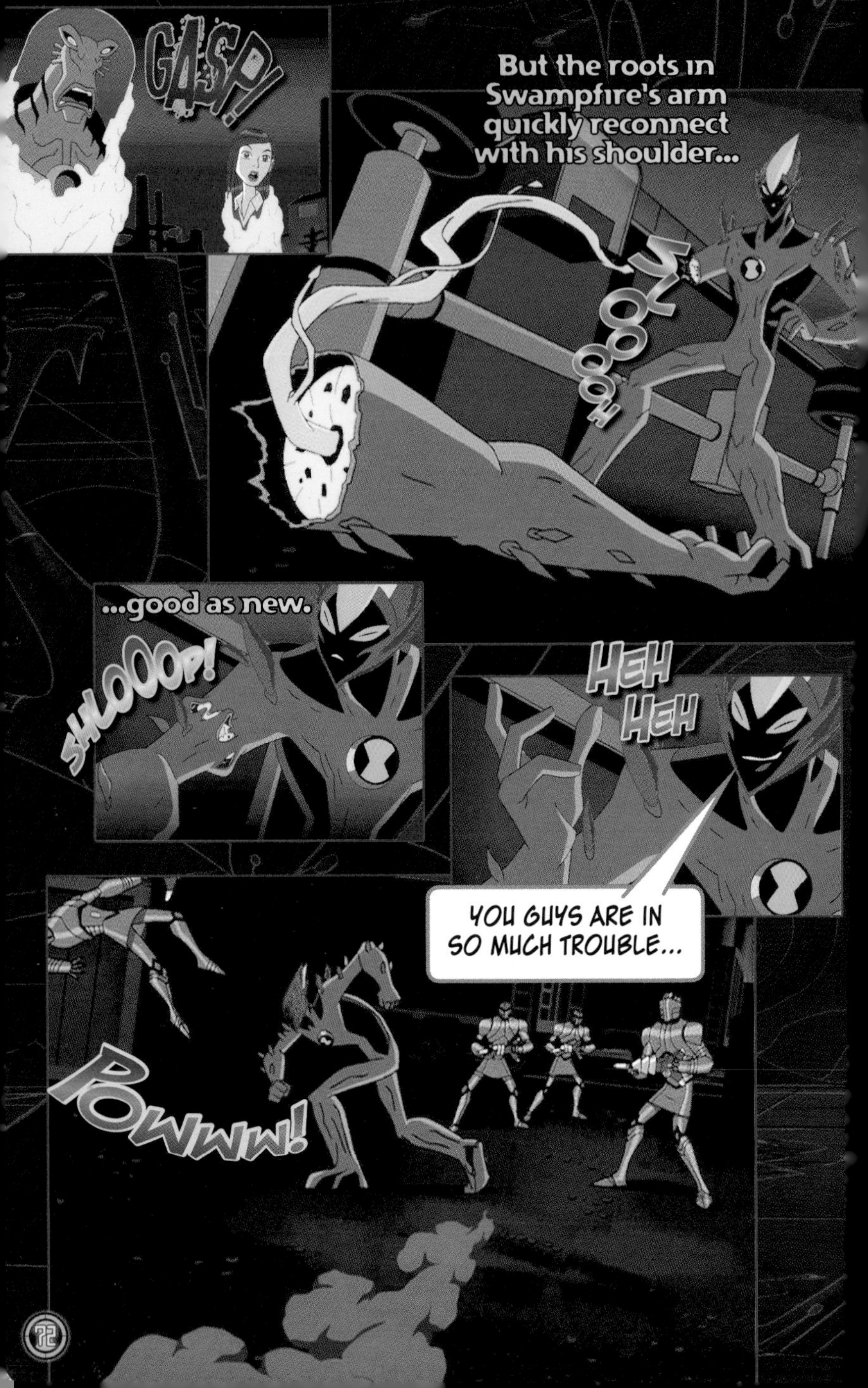

GASP!
But the roots in Swampfire's arm quickly reconnect with his shoulder...
SWOOOOH
...good as new.
SHLOOOP!
HEH HEH
YOU GUYS ARE IN SO MUCH TROUBLE...
POWWW!

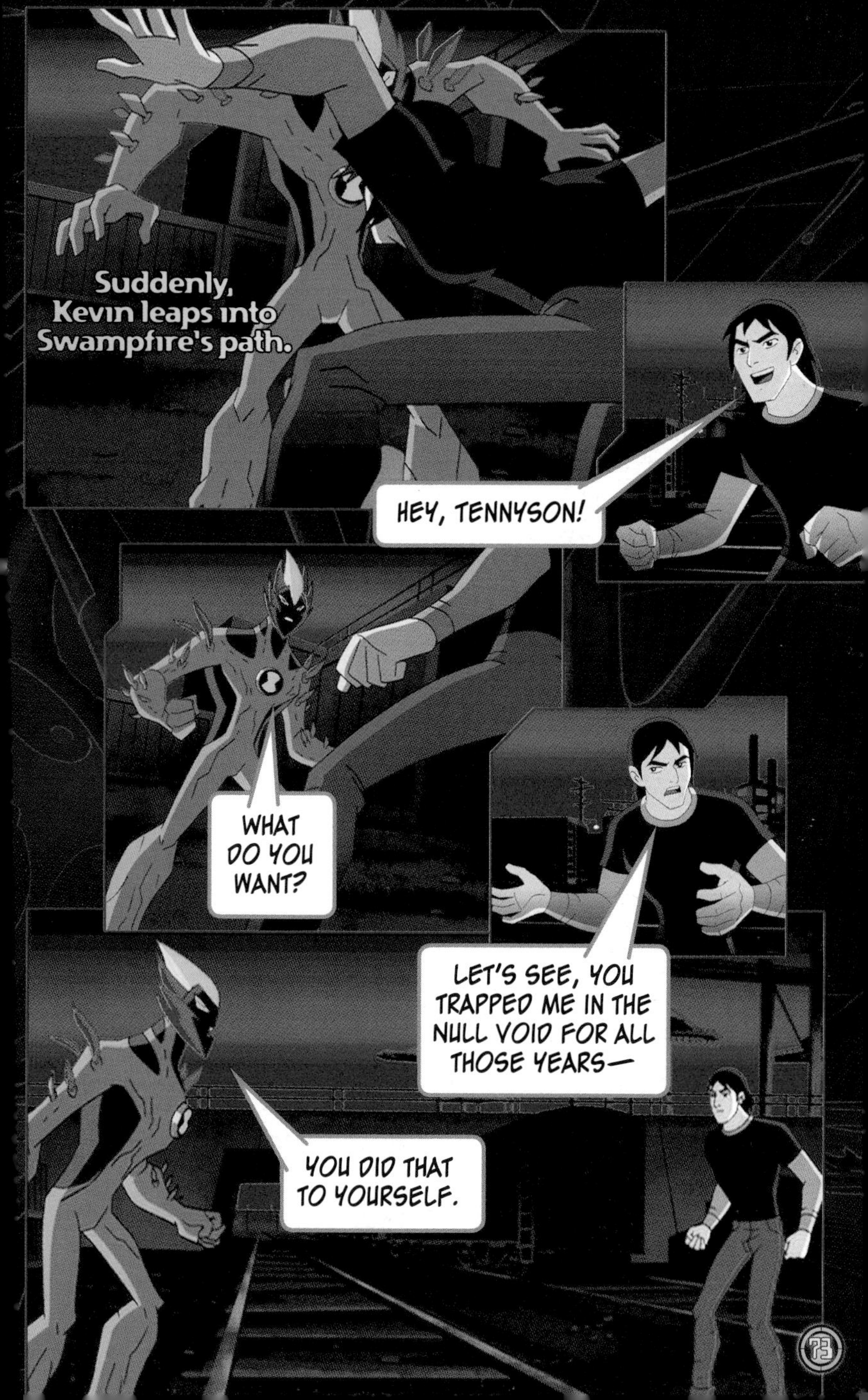
Suddenly, Kevin leaps into Swampfire's path.
HEY, TENNYSON!
WHAT DO YOU WANT?
LET'S SEE, YOU TRAPPED ME IN THE NULL VOID FOR ALL THOSE YEARS—
YOU DID THAT TO YOURSELF.

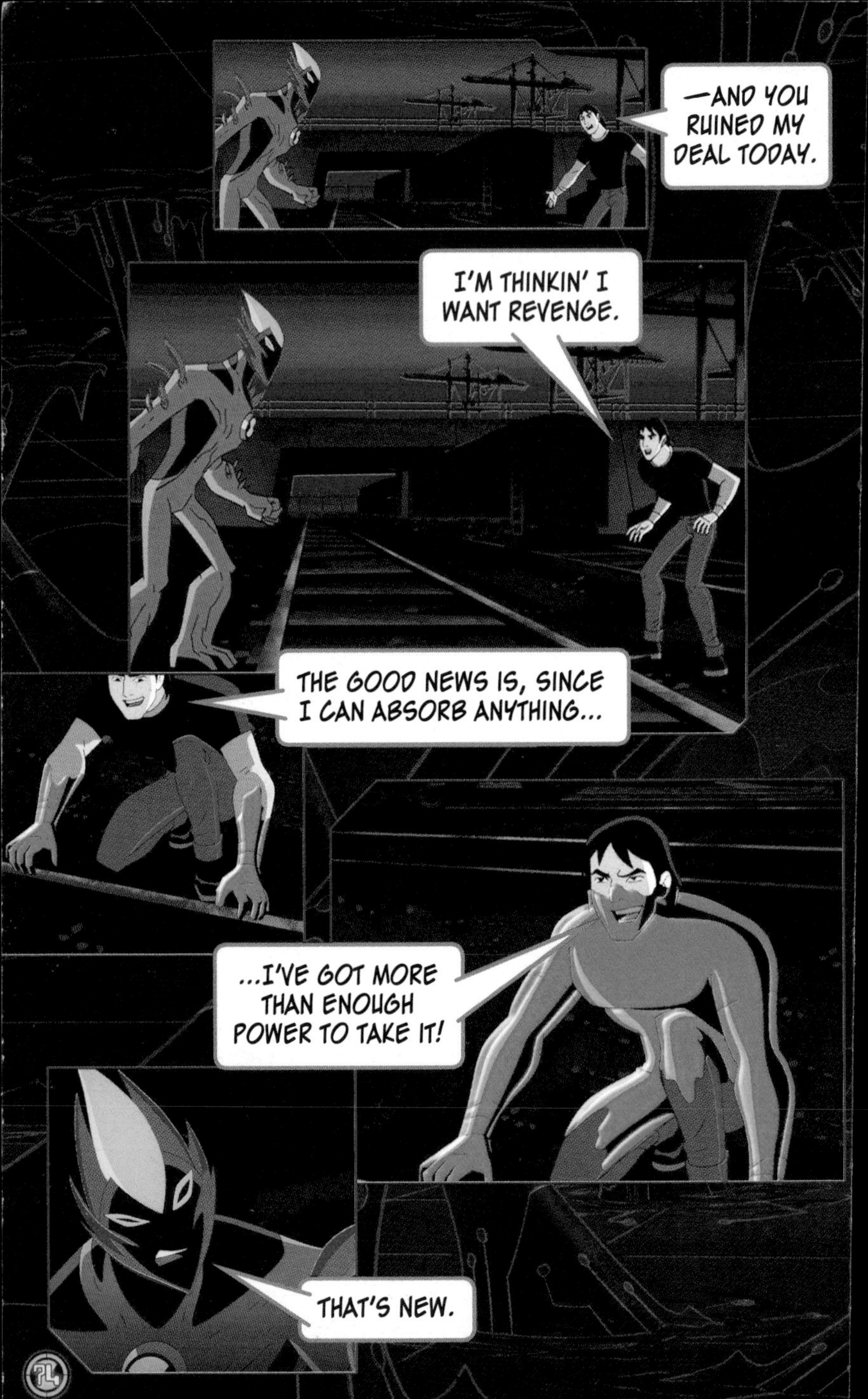
—AND YOU RUINED MY DEAL TODAY.
I'M THINKIN' I WANT REVENGE.
THE GOOD NEWS IS, SINCE I CAN ABSORB ANYTHING...
...I'VE GOT MORE THAN ENOUGH POWER TO TAKE IT!
THAT'S NEW.

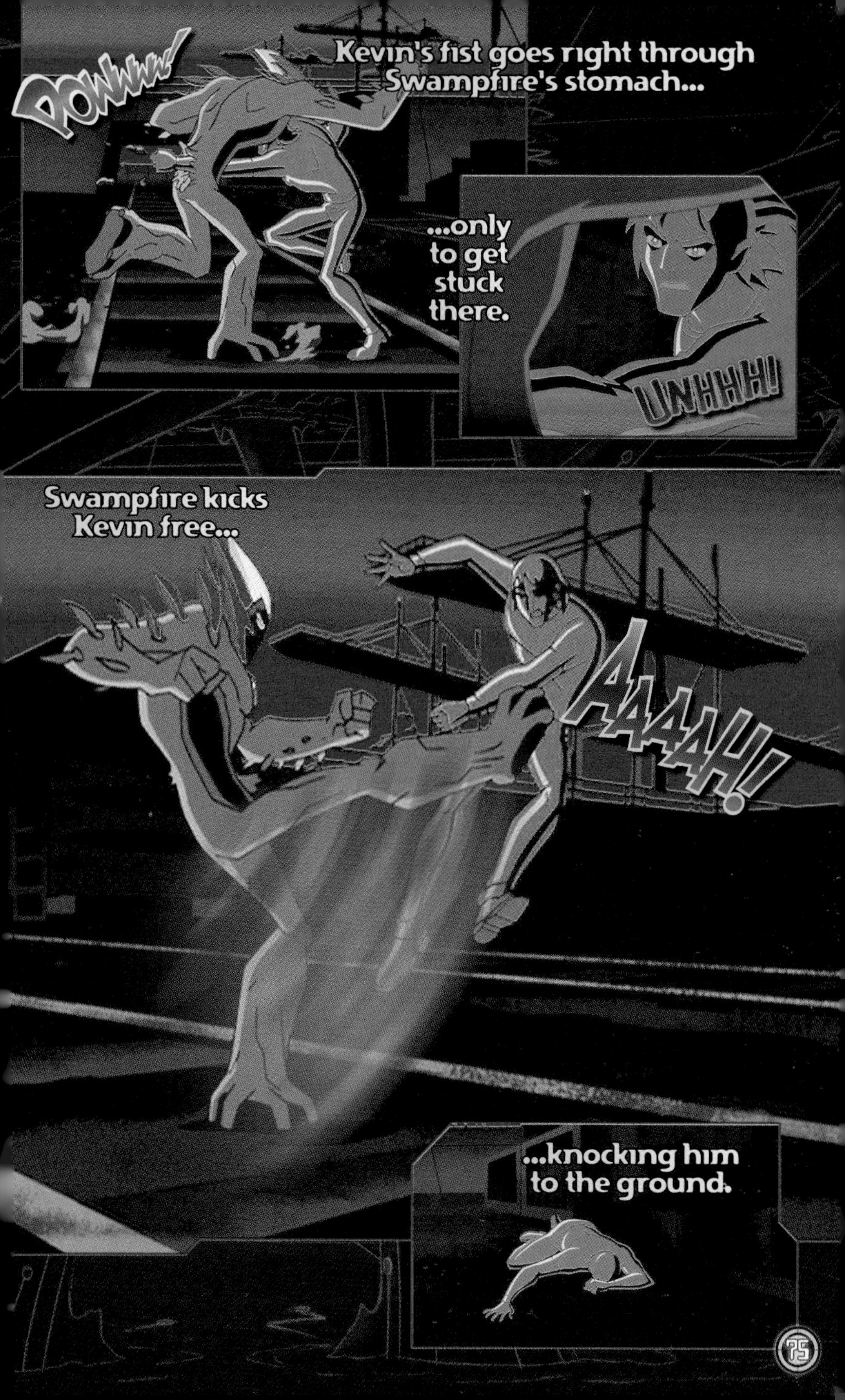
Kevin's fist goes right through Swampfire's stomach...
POWWWW!
...only to get stuck there.
UNHHH!
Swampfire kicks Kevin free...
AAAAH!
...knocking him to the ground.

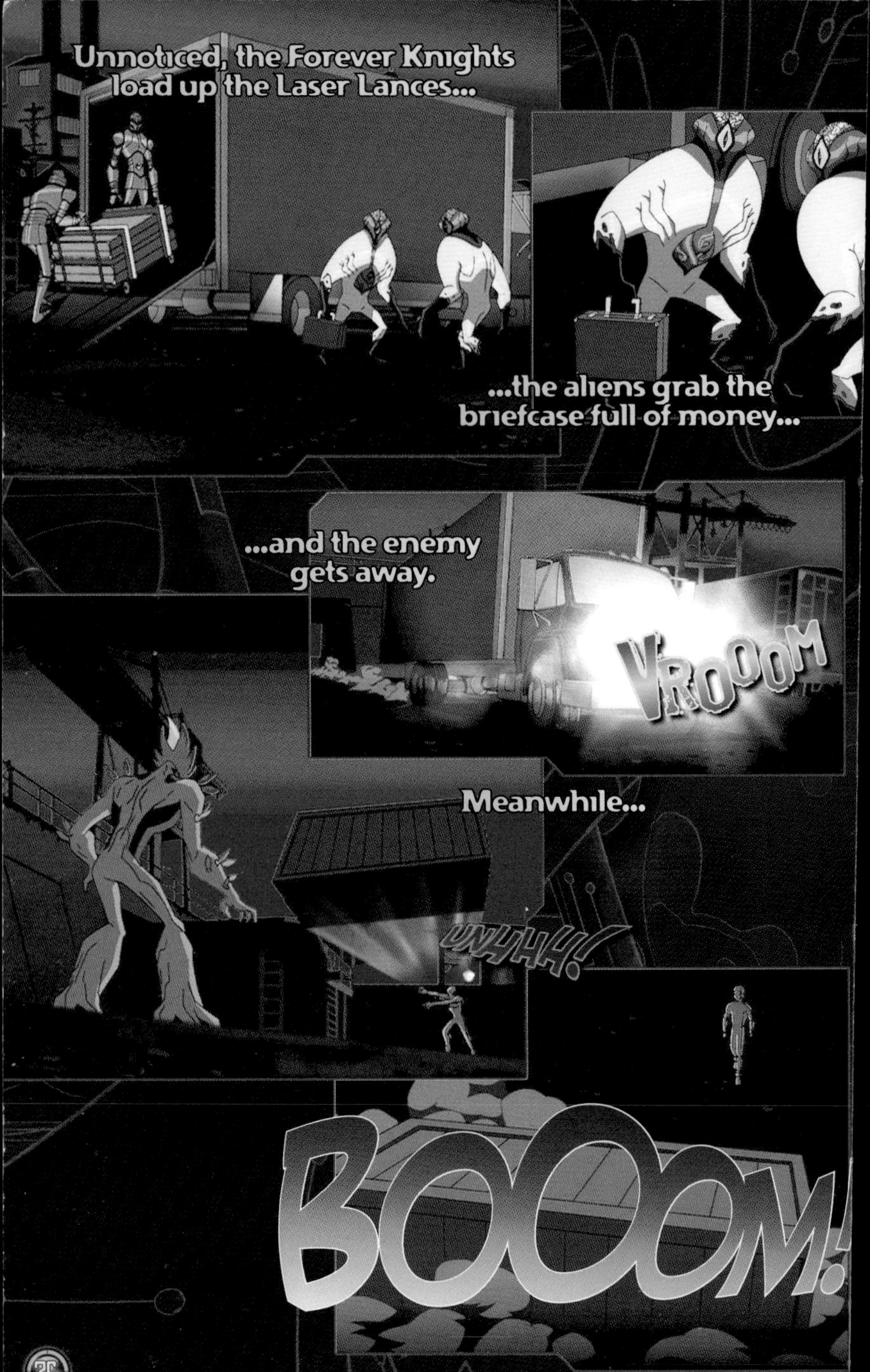
Unnoticed, the Forever Knights load up the Laser Lances...
...the aliens grab the briefcase full of money...
...and the enemy gets away.
VROOOM
Meanwhile...
UNGHH!
BOOOM!

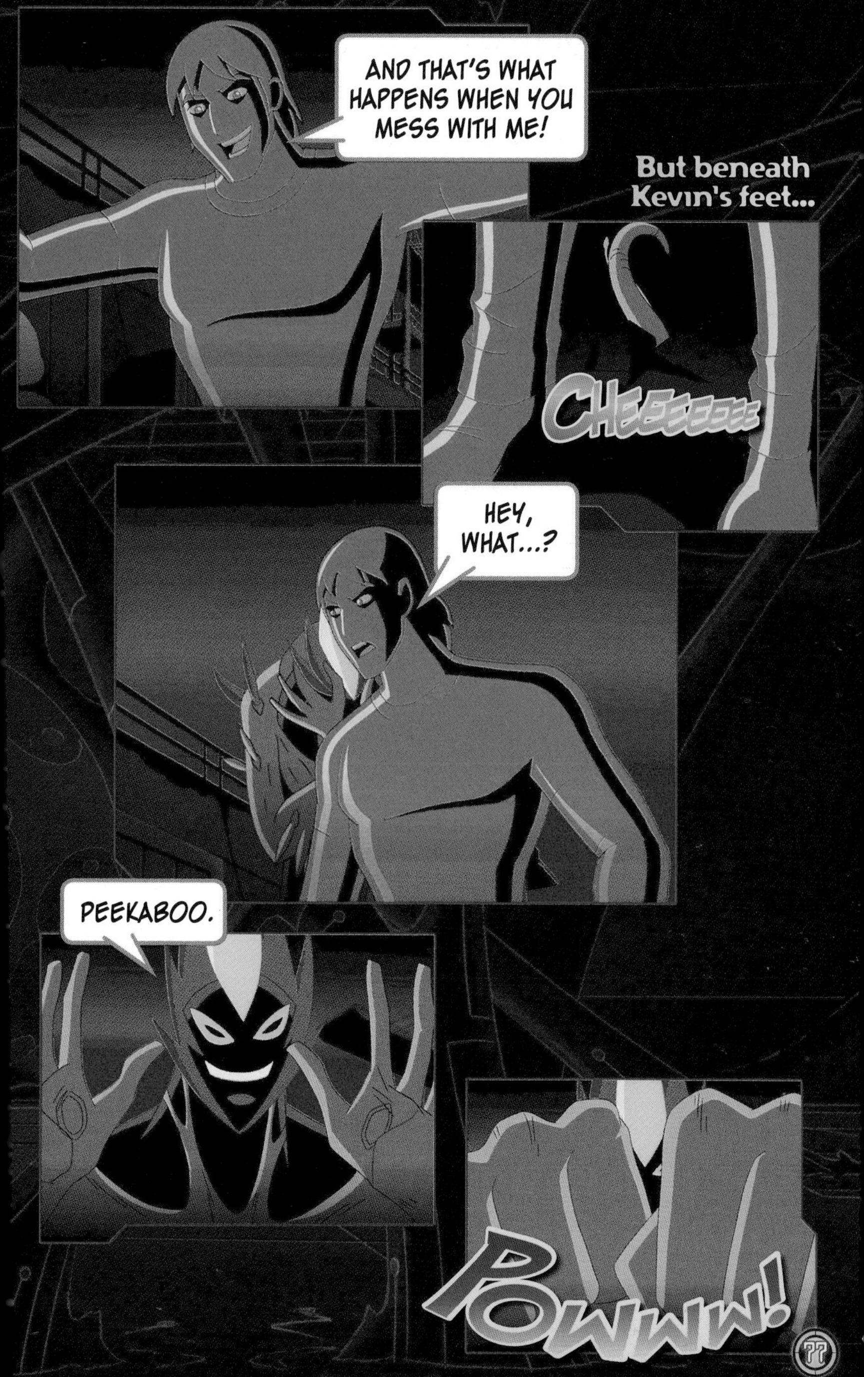
AND THAT'S WHAT HAPPENS WHEN YOU MESS WITH ME!
But beneath Kevin's feet...
CHEEEEEEE
HEY, WHAT...?
PEEKABOO.
POWWW!

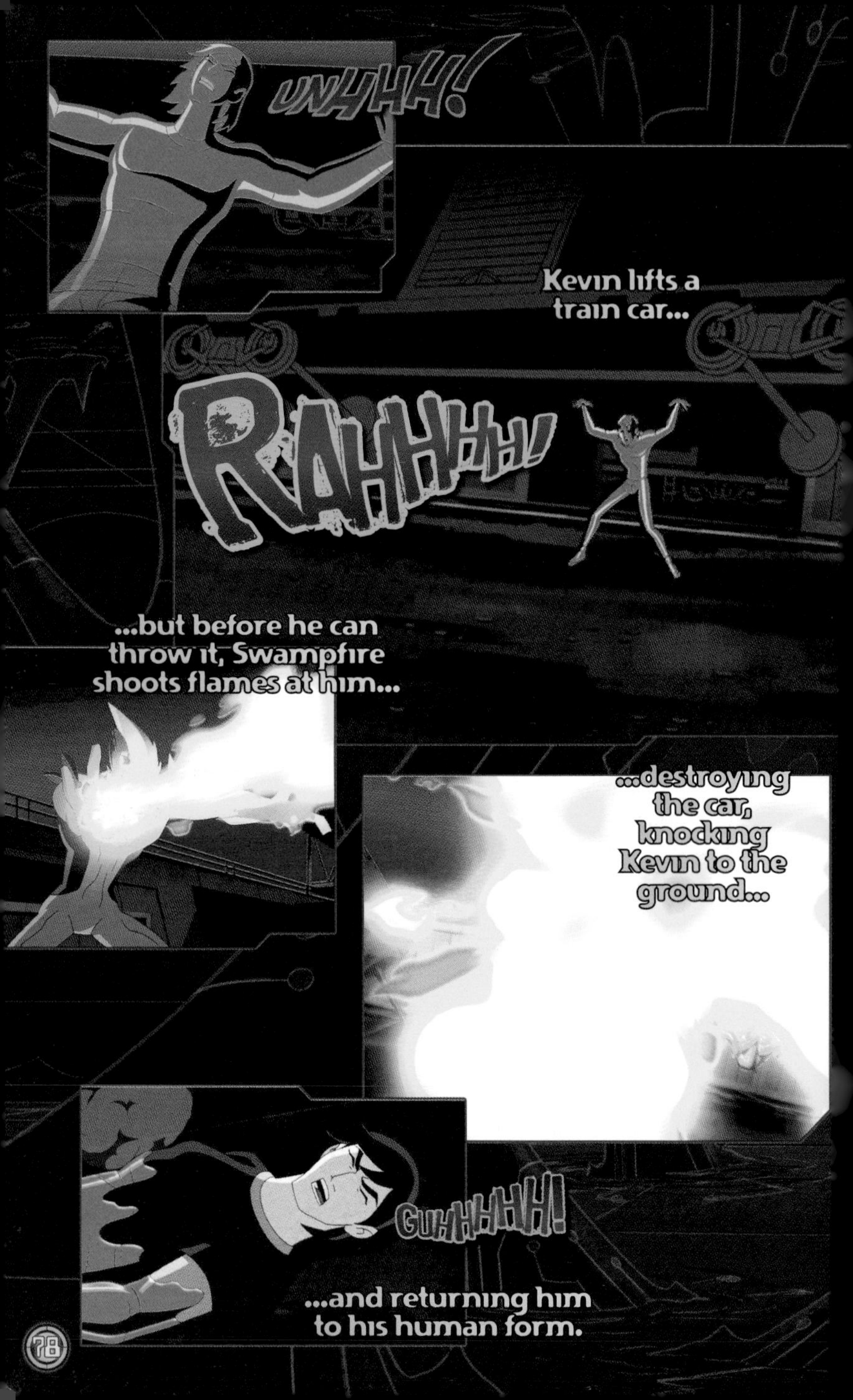
UNHHH!
Kevin lifts a train car...
RAHHHHH!
...but before he can throw it, Swampfire shoots flames at him...
...destroying the car, knocking Kevin to the ground...
GUHHHHHH!
...and returning him to his human form.

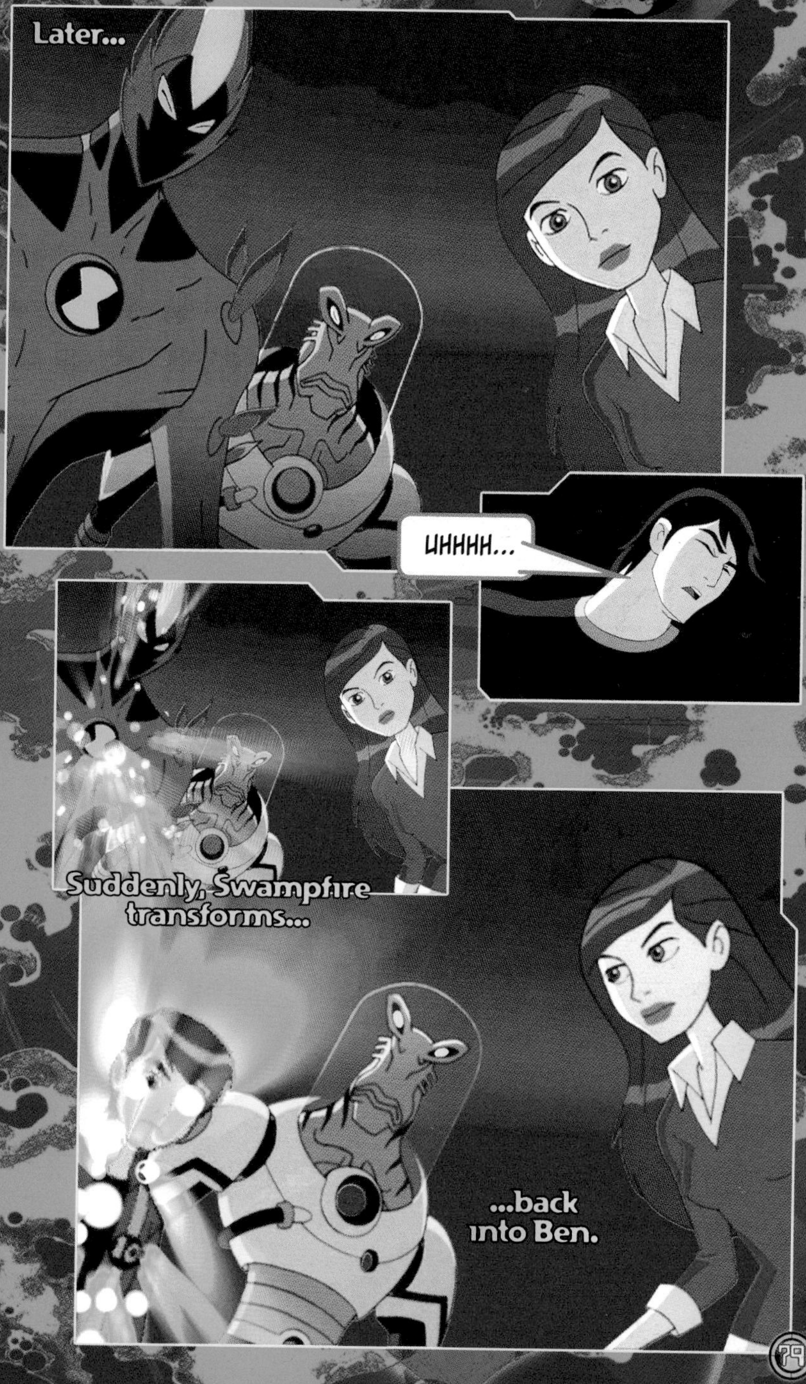

Later...
UHHHH...
Suddenly, Swampfire transforms...
...back into Ben.

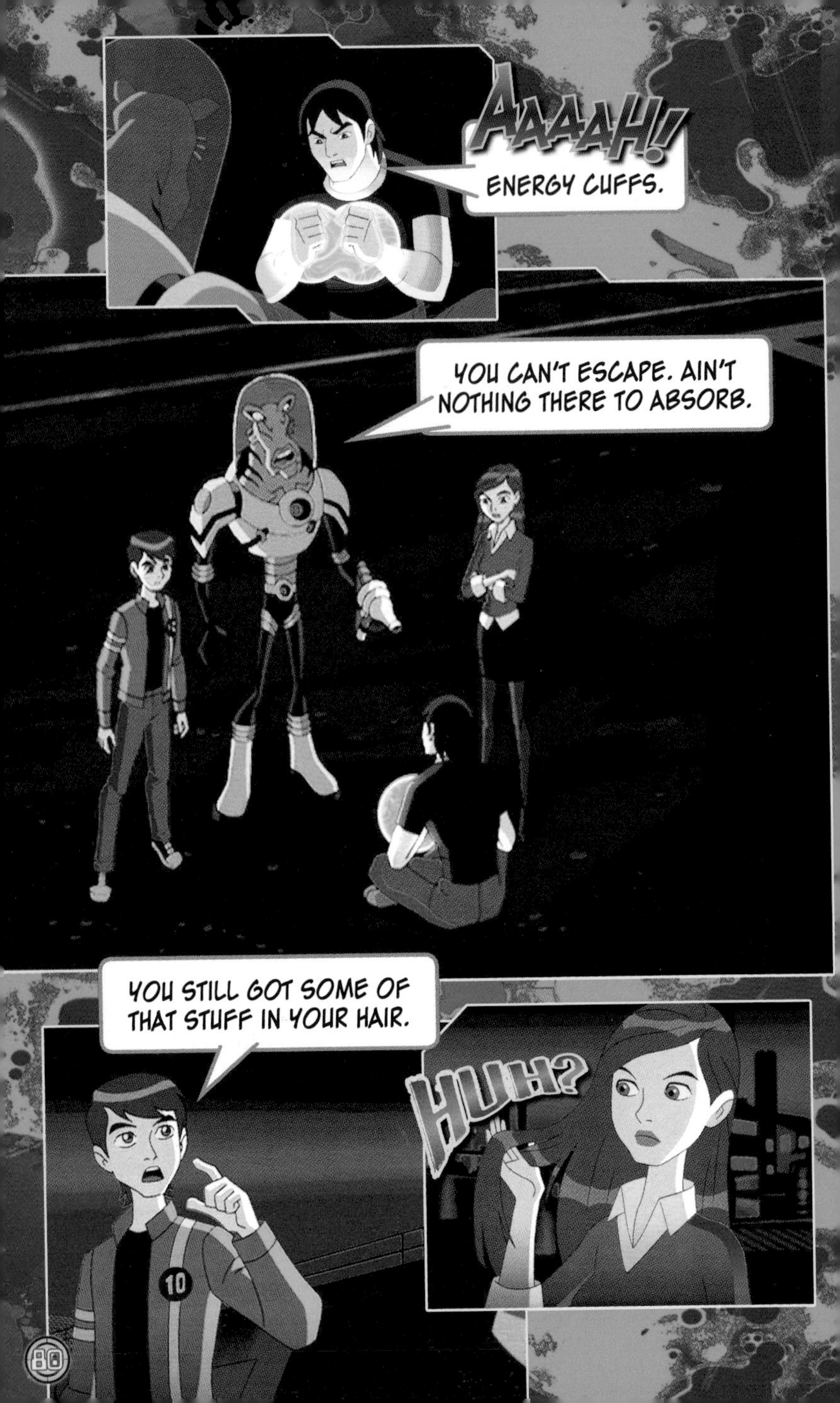
AAAAH!
ENERGY CUFFS.
YOU CAN'T ESCAPE. AIN'T NOTHING THERE TO ABSORB.
YOU STILL GOT SOME OF THAT STUFF IN YOUR HAIR.
HUH?
10

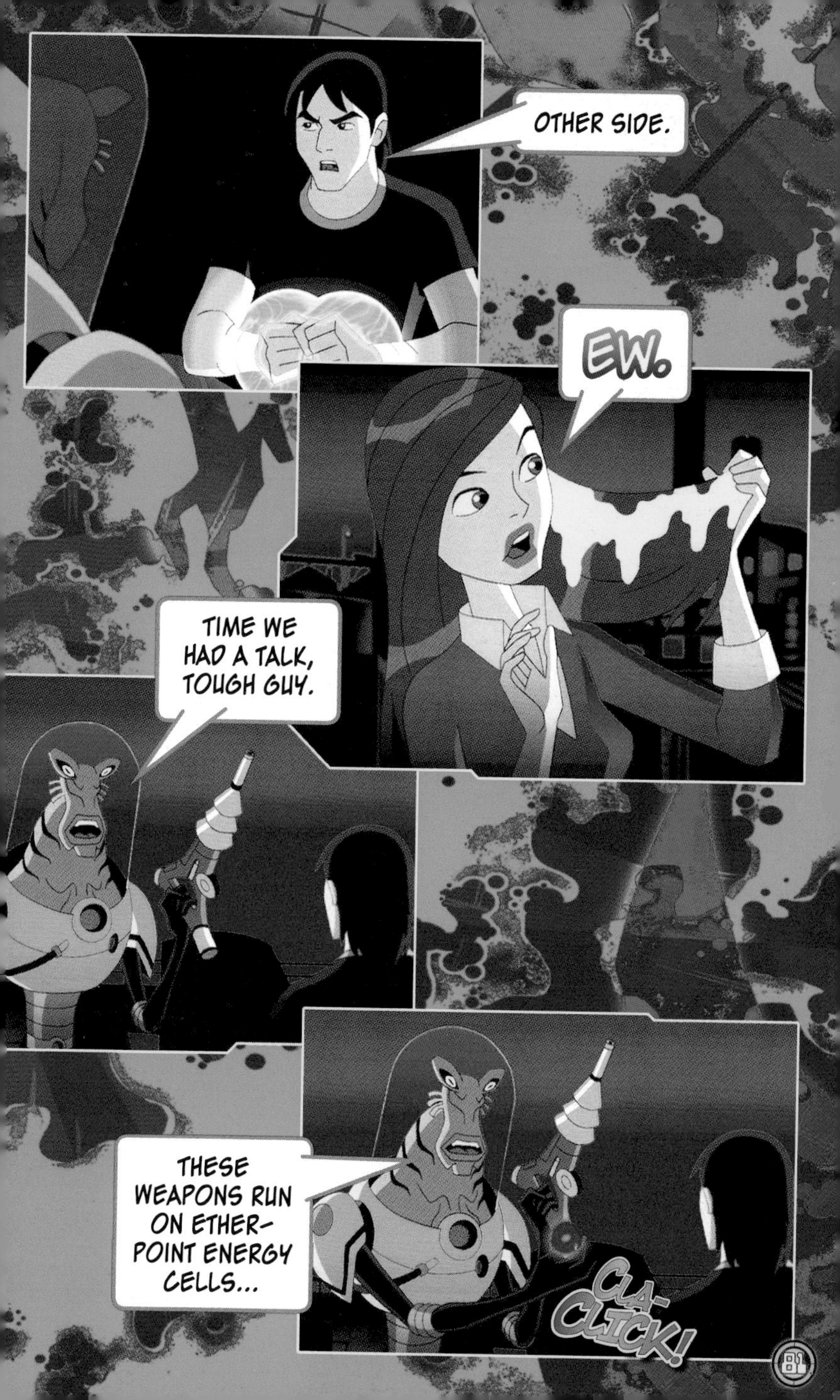
OTHER SIDE.
EW.
TIME WE HAD A TALK, TOUGH GUY.
THESE WEAPONS RUN ON ETHER-POINT ENERGY CELLS...
CLA-CLICK!

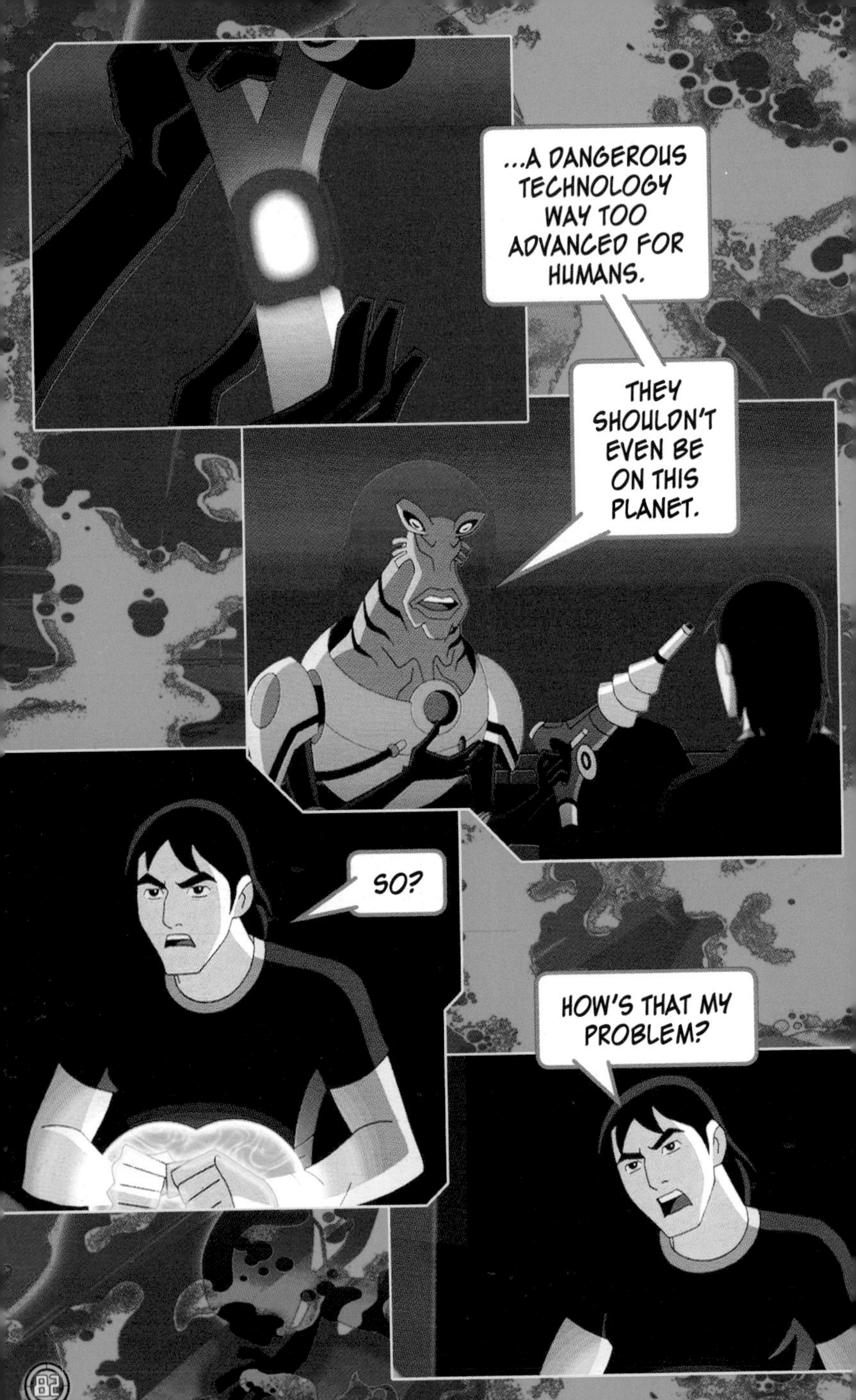
...A DANGEROUS TECHNOLOGY WAY TOO ADVANCED FOR HUMANS.
THEY SHOULDN'T EVEN BE ON THIS PLANET.
SO?
HOW'S THAT MY PROBLEM?

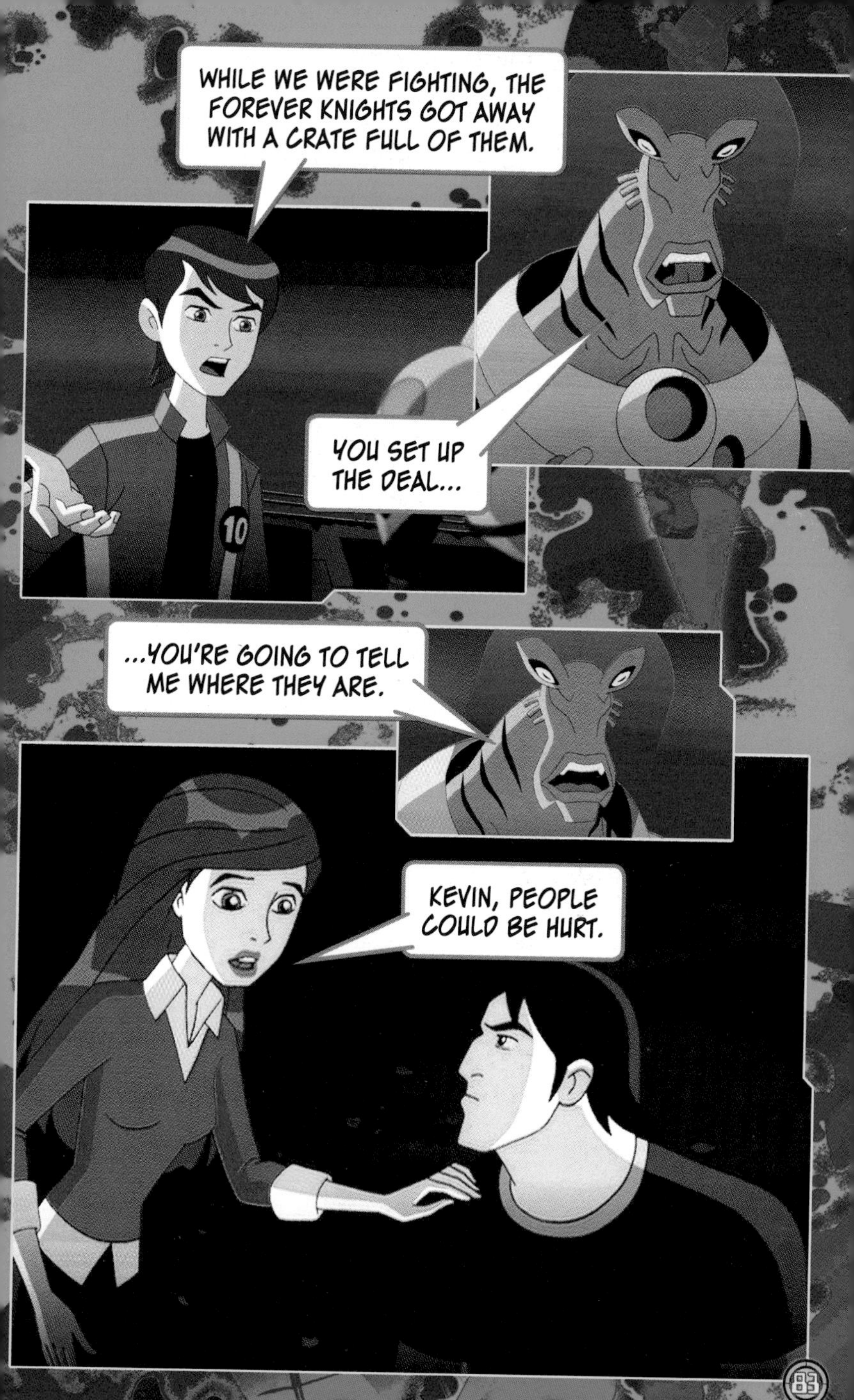
WHILE WE WERE FIGHTING, THE FOREVER KNIGHTS GOT AWAY WITH A CRATE FULL OF THEM.
YOU SET UP THE DEAL...
...YOU'RE GOING TO TELL ME WHERE THEY ARE.
KEVIN, PEOPLE COULD BE HURT.

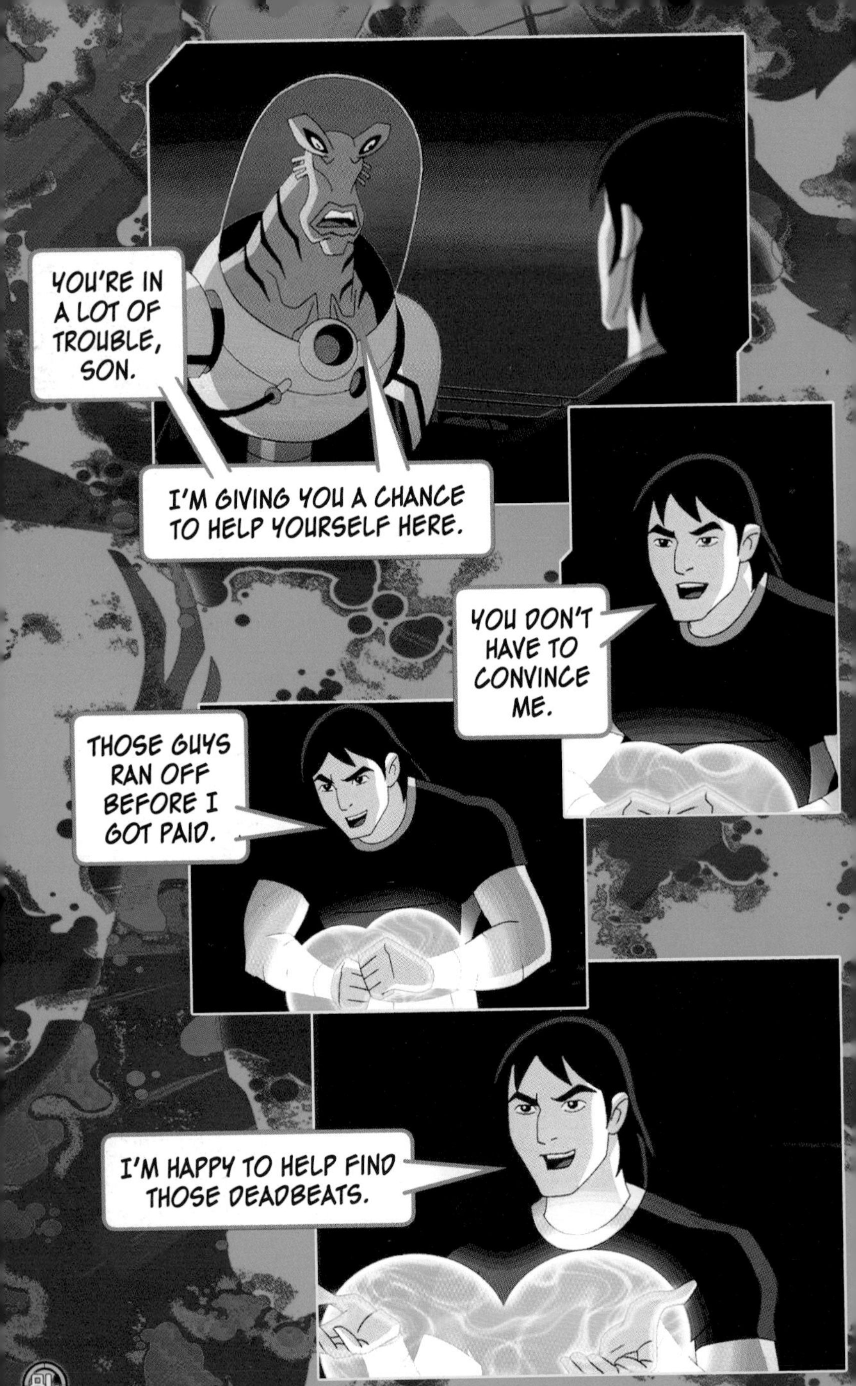
YOU'RE IN A LOT OF TROUBLE, SON.
I'M GIVING YOU A CHANCE TO HELP YOURSELF HERE.
YOU DON'T HAVE TO CONVINCE ME.
THOSE GUYS RAN OFF BEFORE I GOT PAID.
I'M HAPPY TO HELP FIND THOSE DEADBEATS.

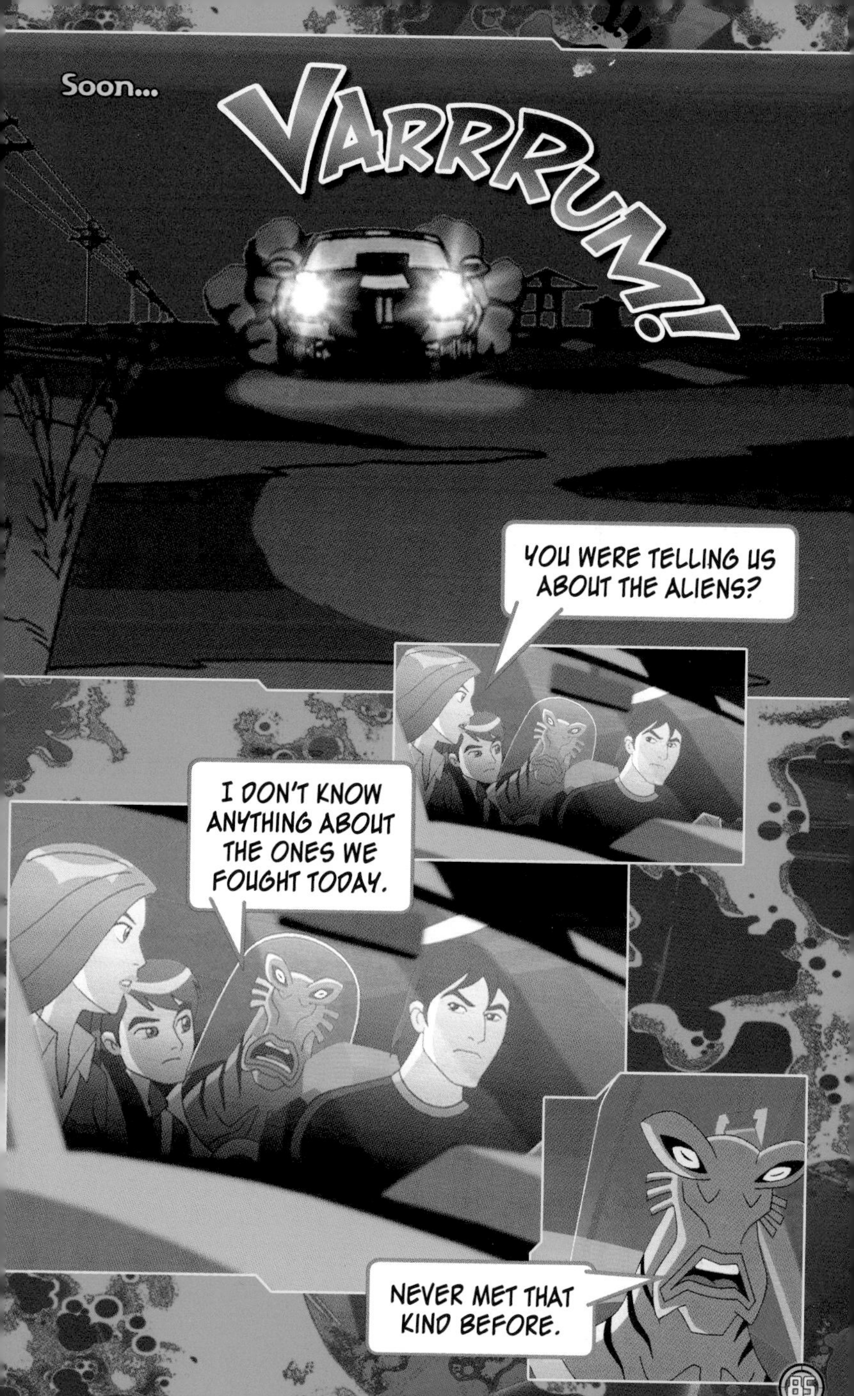
Soon...
VARRRUM!
YOU WERE TELLING US ABOUT THE ALIENS?
I DON'T KNOW ANYTHING ABOUT THE ONES WE FOUGHT TODAY.
NEVER MET THAT KIND BEFORE.

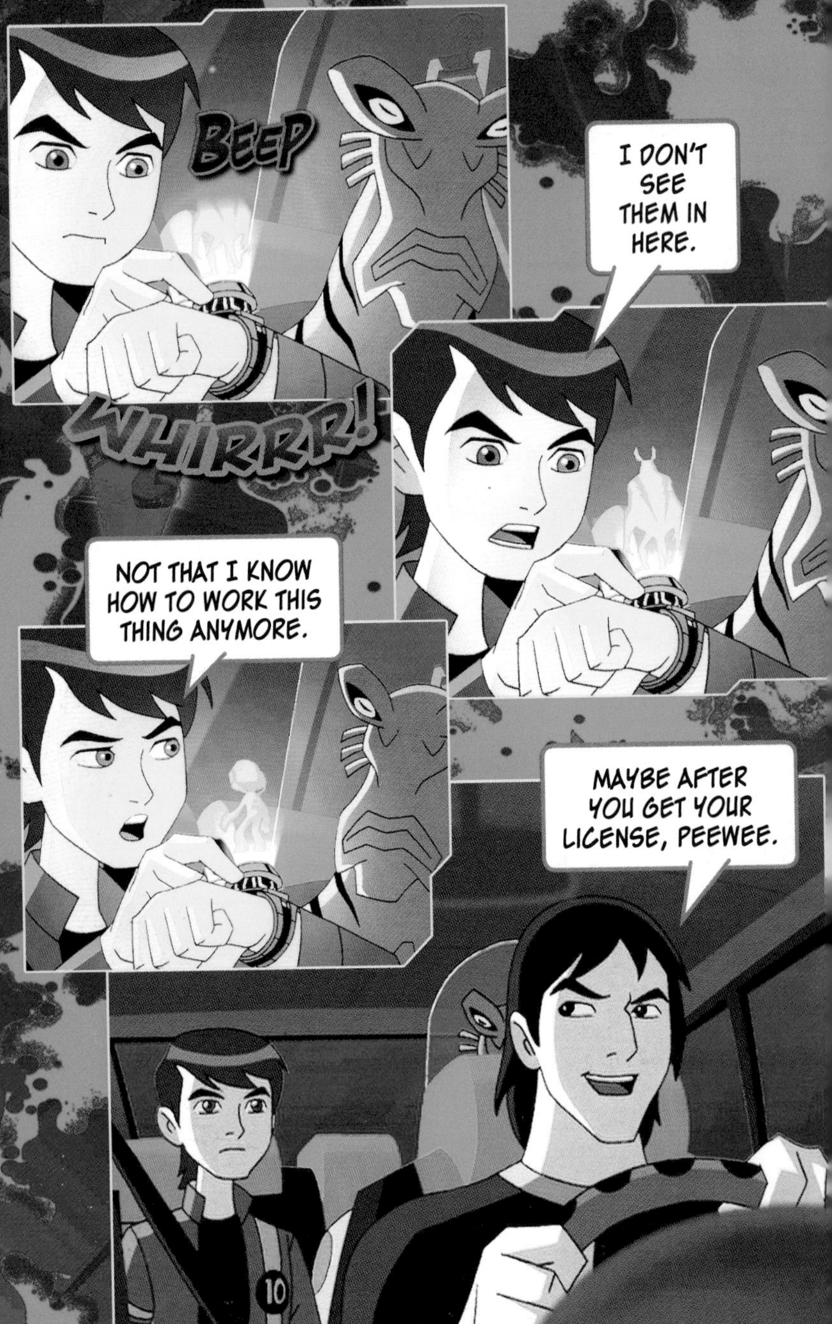
BEEP
WHIRRR!
I DON'T SEE THEM IN HERE.
NOT THAT I KNOW HOW TO WORK THIS THING ANYMORE.
MAYBE AFTER YOU GET YOUR LICENSE, PEEWEE.
10

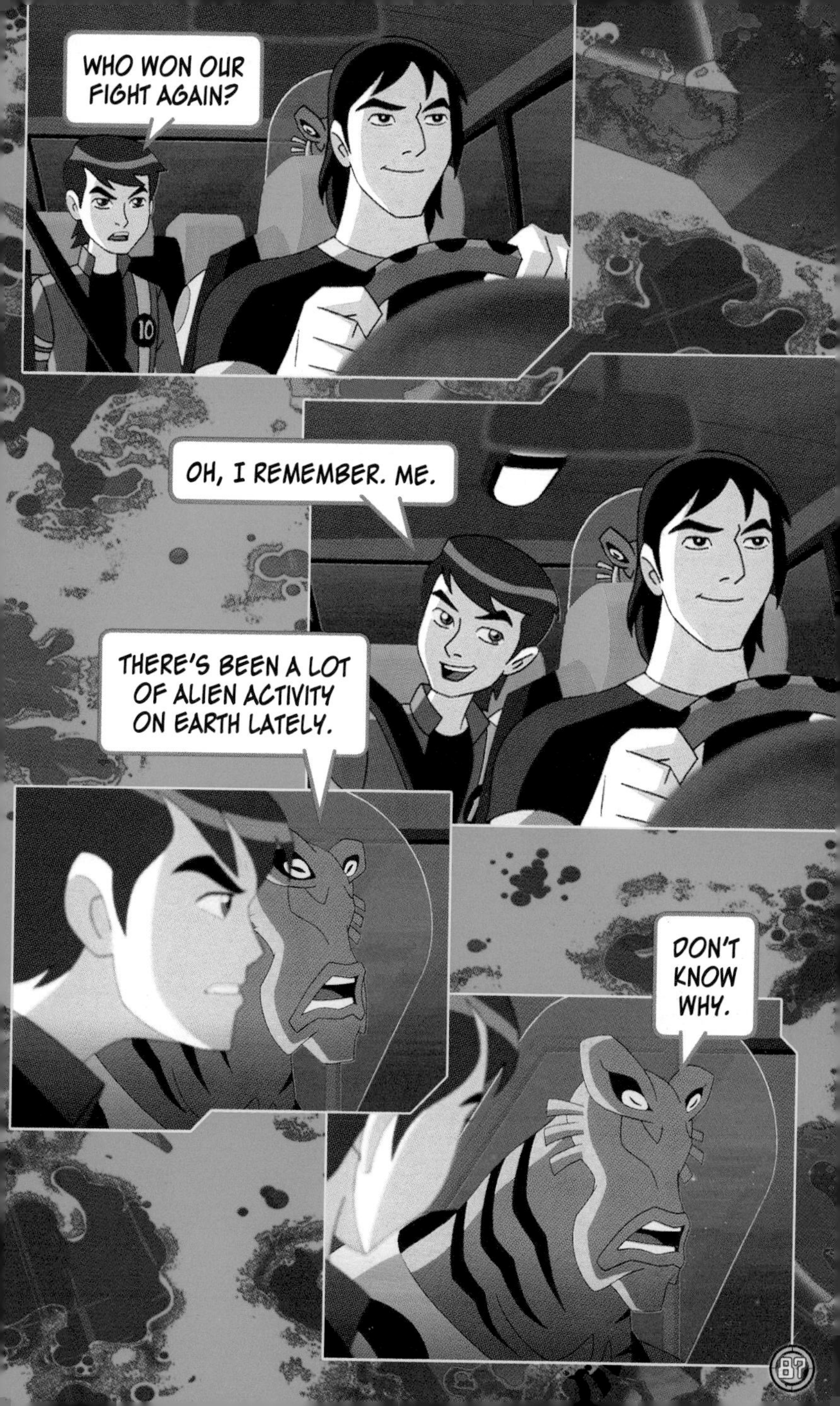
WHO WON OUR FIGHT AGAIN?
OH, I REMEMBER. ME.
THERE'S BEEN A LOT OF ALIEN ACTIVITY ON EARTH LATELY.
DON'T KNOW WHY.

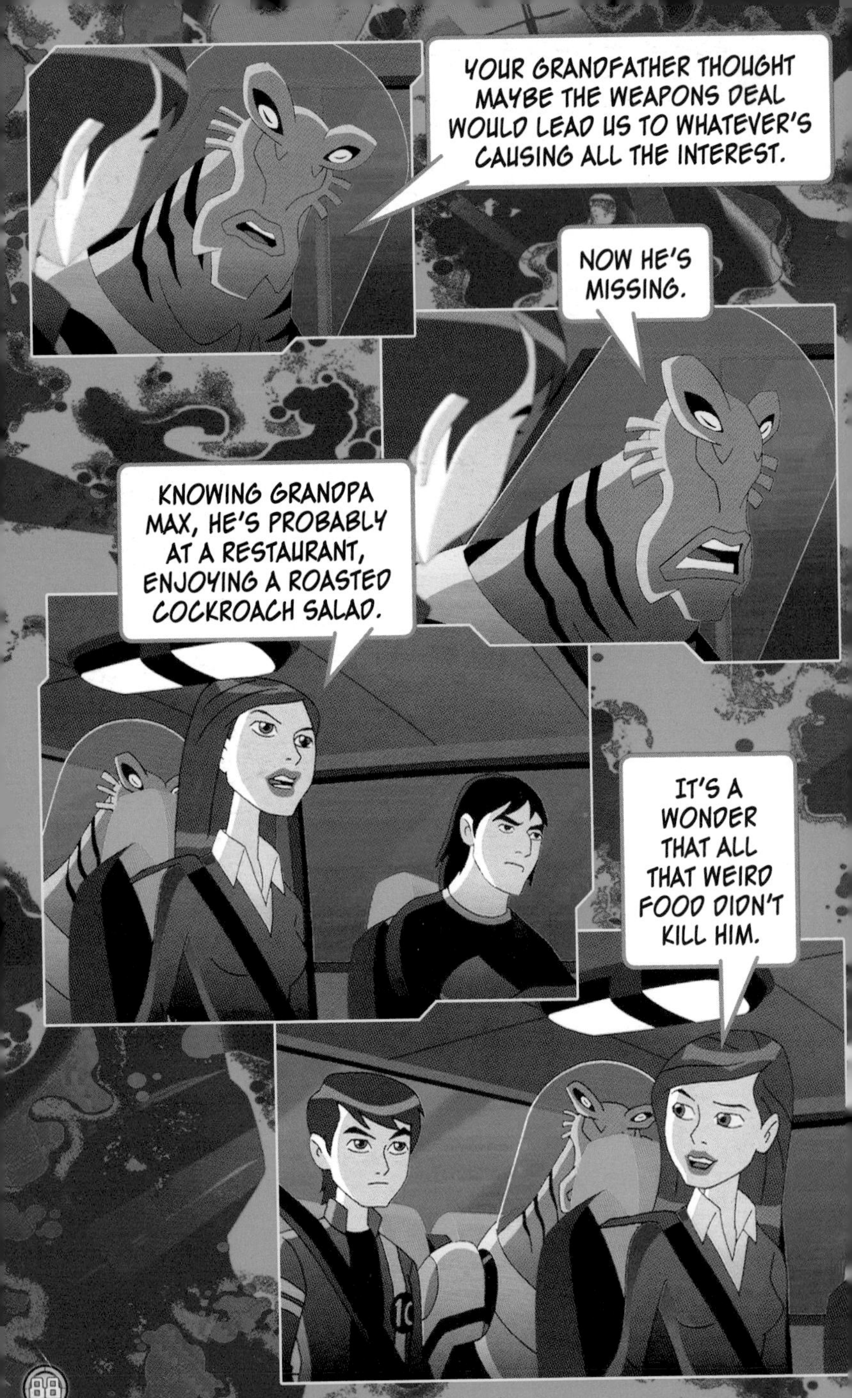
YOUR GRANDFATHER THOUGHT MAYBE THE WEAPONS DEAL WOULD LEAD US TO WHATEVER'S CAUSING ALL THE INTEREST.
NOW HE'S MISSING.
KNOWING GRANDPA MAX, HE'S PROBABLY AT A RESTAURANT, ENJOYING A ROASTED COCKROACH SALAD.
IT'S A WONDER THAT ALL THAT WEIRD FOOD DIDN'T KILL HIM.

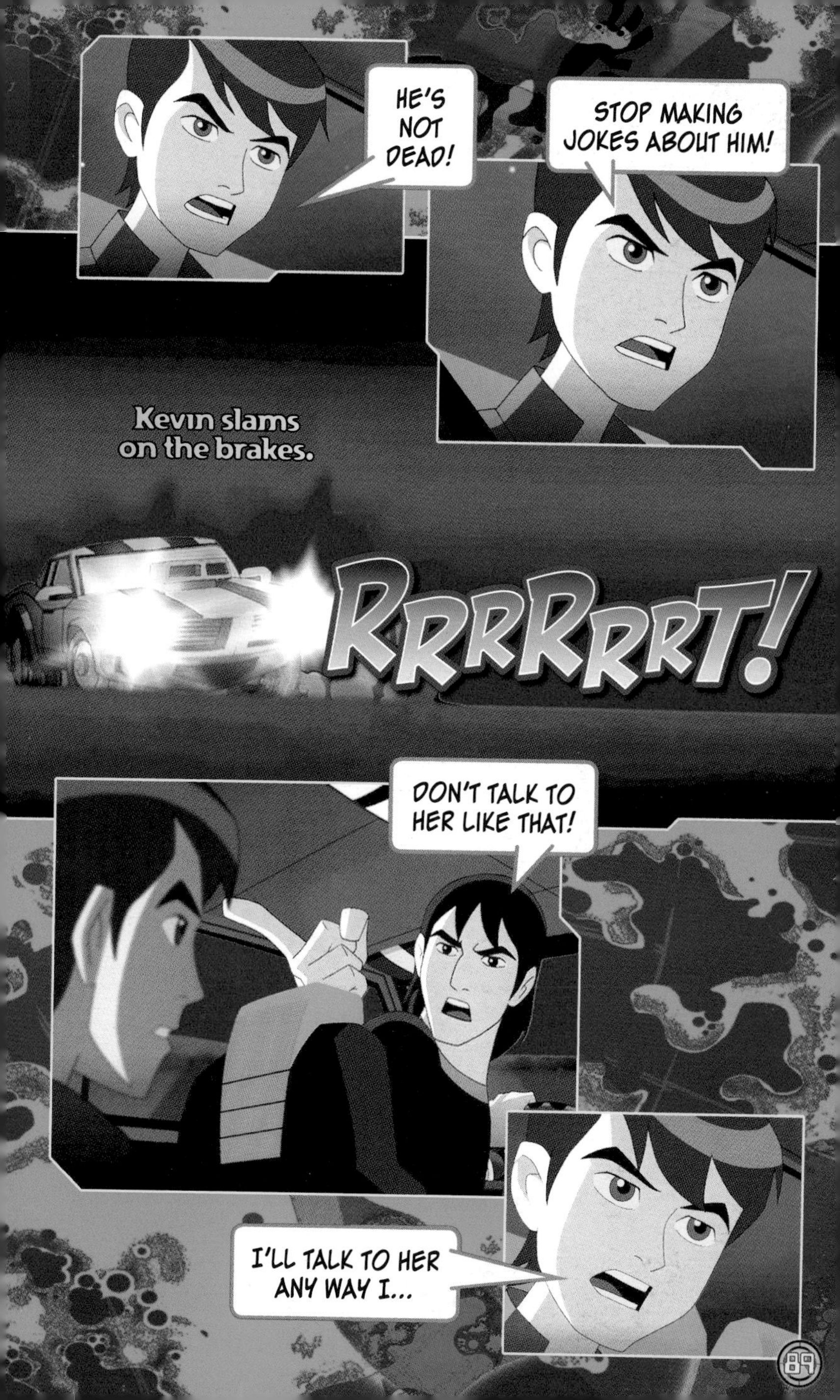
HE'S NOT DEAD!
STOP MAKING JOKES ABOUT HIM!
Kevin slams on the brakes.
RRRRRRT!
DON'T TALK TO HER LIKE THAT!
I'LL TALK TO HER ANY WAY I...

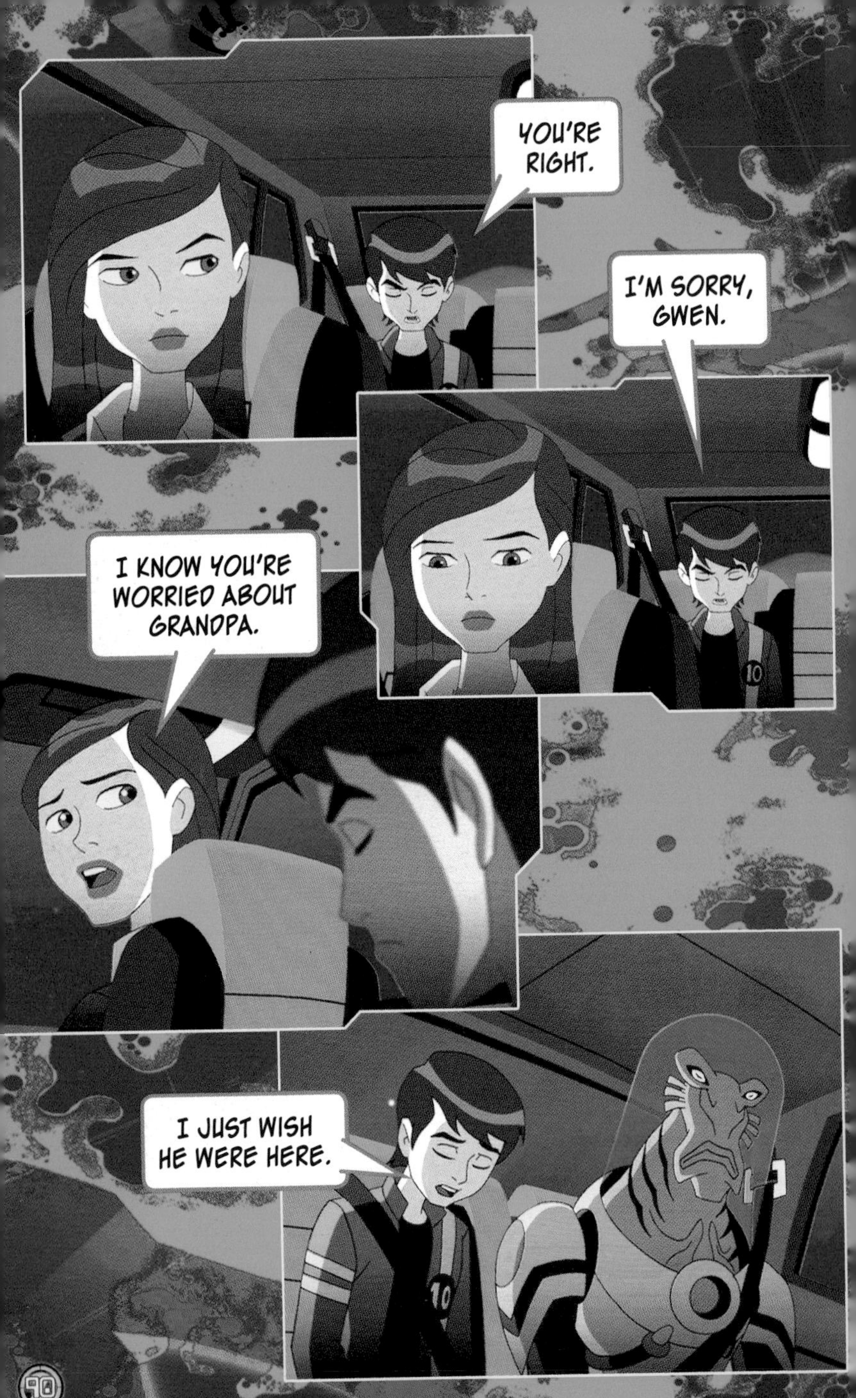
YOU'RE RIGHT.
I'M SORRY, GWEN.
I KNOW YOU'RE WORRIED ABOUT GRANDPA.
I JUST WISH HE WERE HERE.

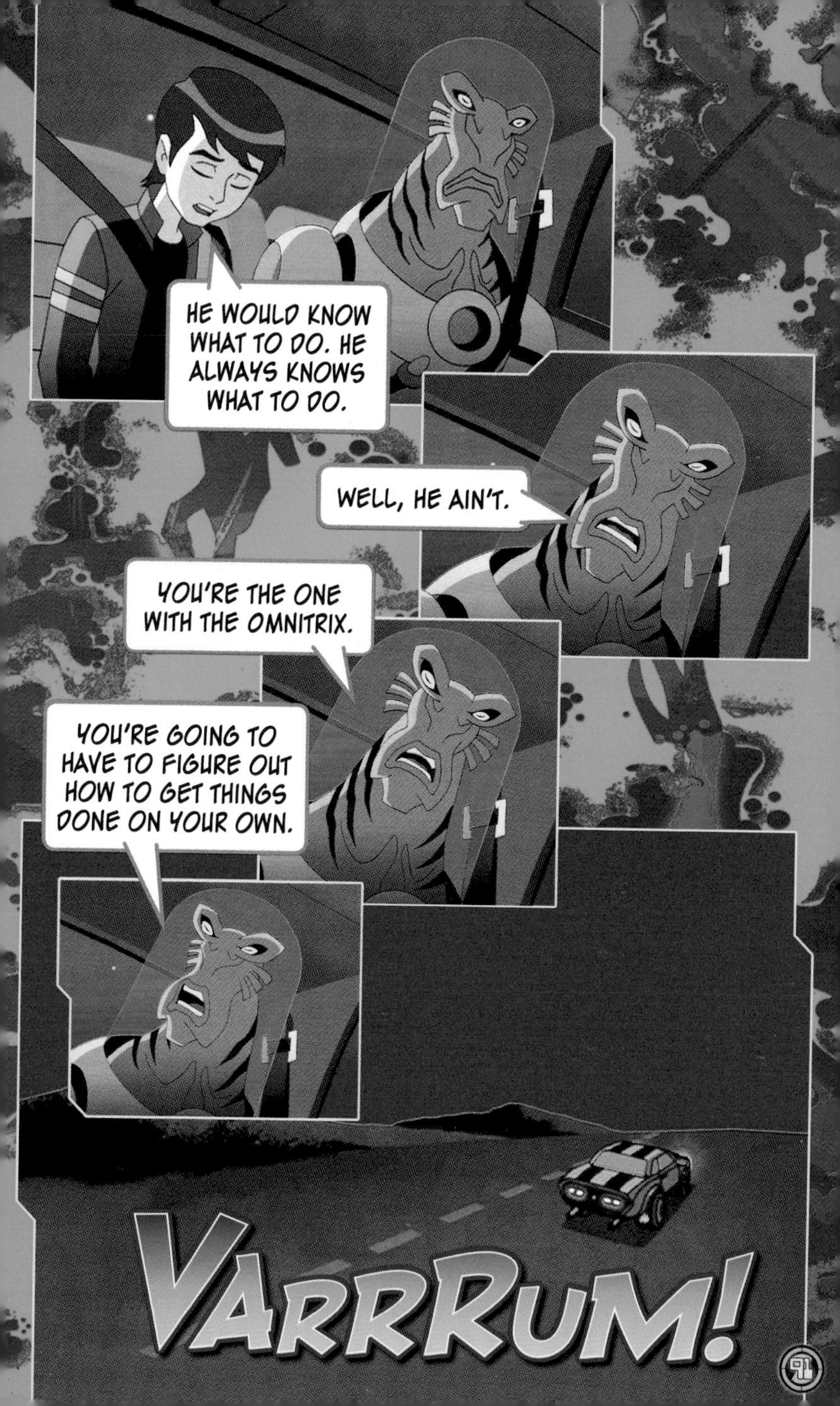

HE WOULD KNOW WHAT TO DO. HE ALWAYS KNOWS WHAT TO DO.
WELL, HE AIN'T.
YOU'RE THE ONE WITH THE OMNITRIX.
YOU'RE GOING TO HAVE TO FIGURE OUT HOW TO GET THINGS DONE ON YOUR OWN.
VARRRUM!

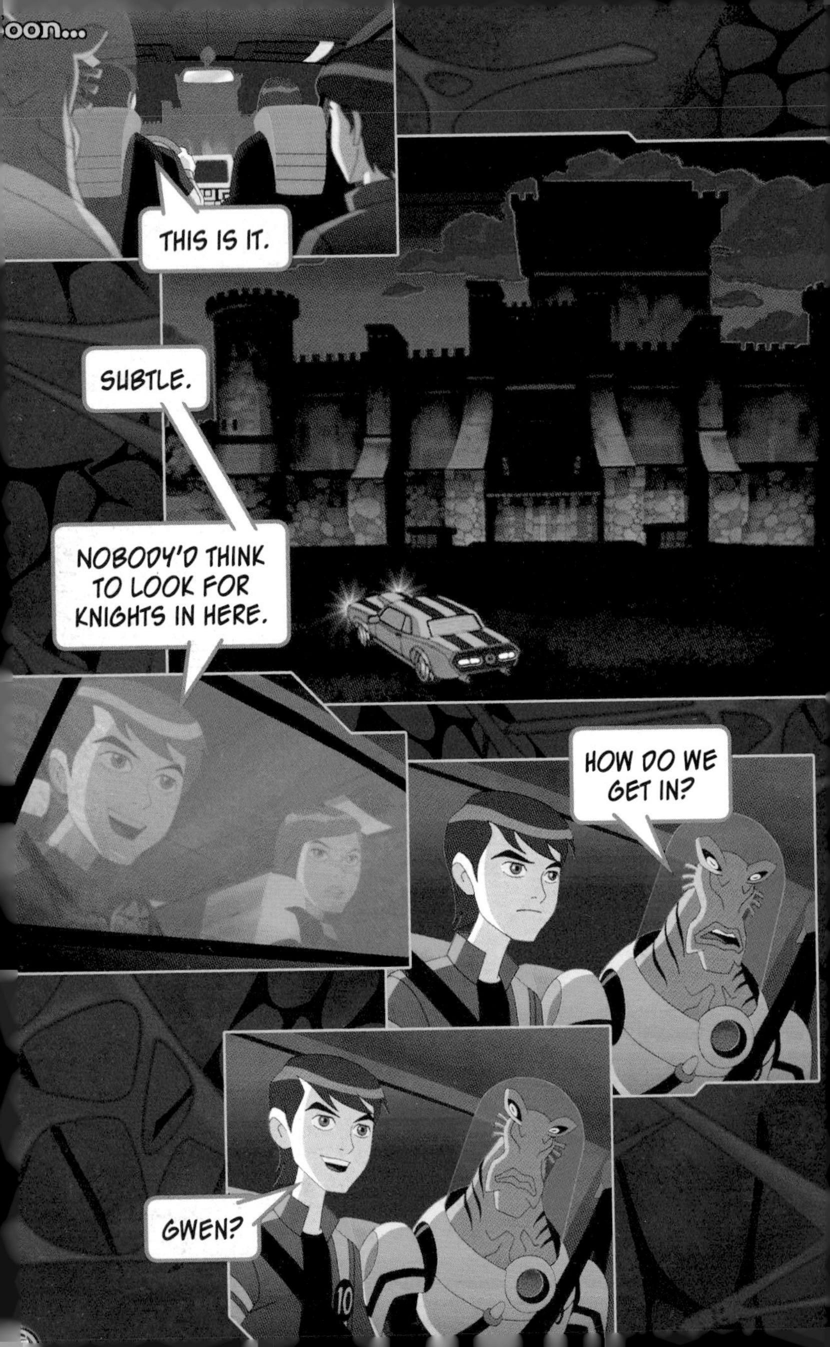
...oon...
THIS IS IT.
SUBTLE.
NOBODY'D THINK TO LOOK FOR KNIGHTS IN HERE.
HOW DO WE GET IN?
GWEN?

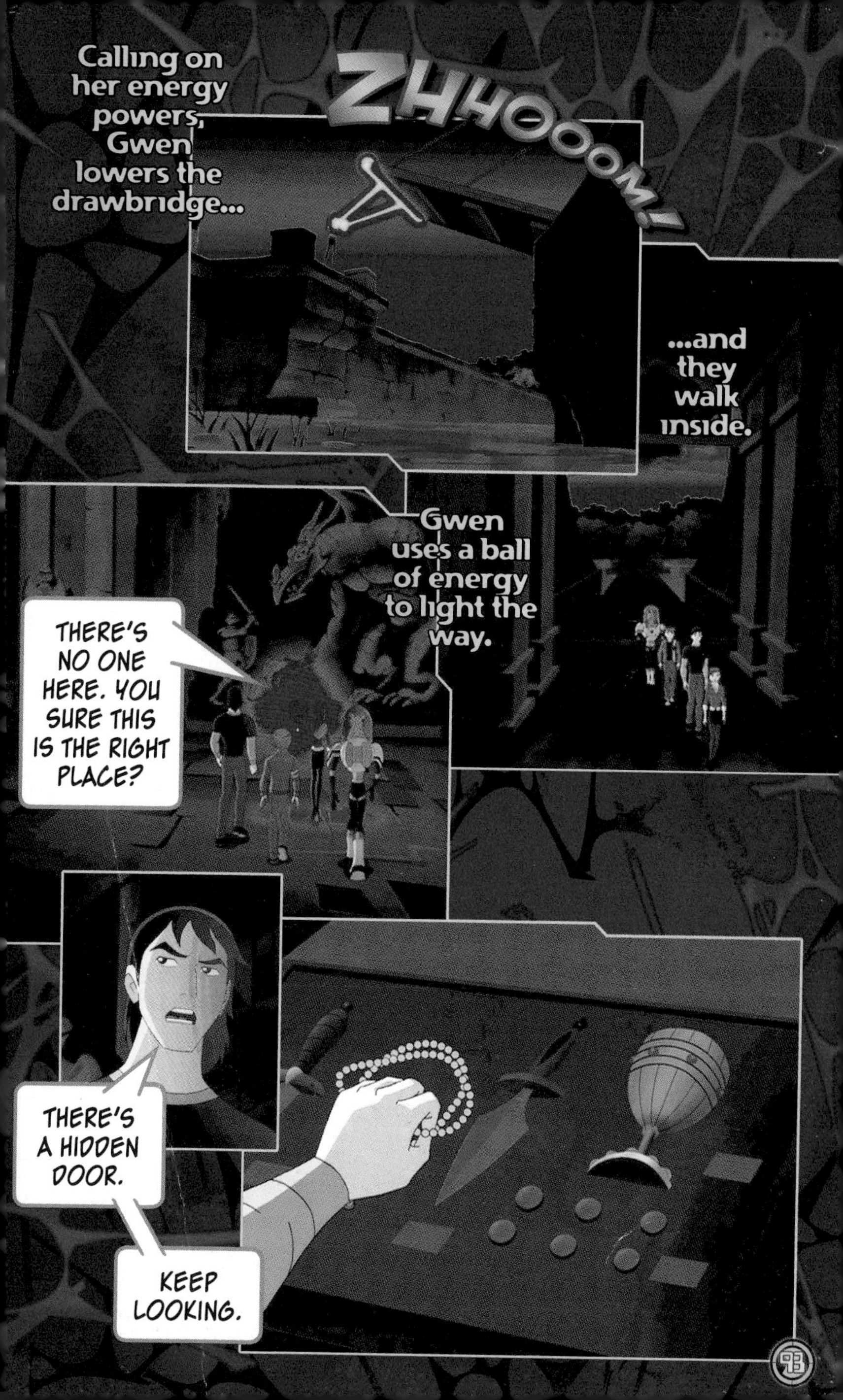
Calling on her energy powers, Gwen lowers the drawbridge...
ZHHOOOM!
...and they walk inside.
Gwen uses a ball of energy to light the way.
THERE'S NO ONE HERE. YOU SURE THIS IS THE RIGHT PLACE?
THERE'S A HIDDEN DOOR.
KEEP LOOKING.

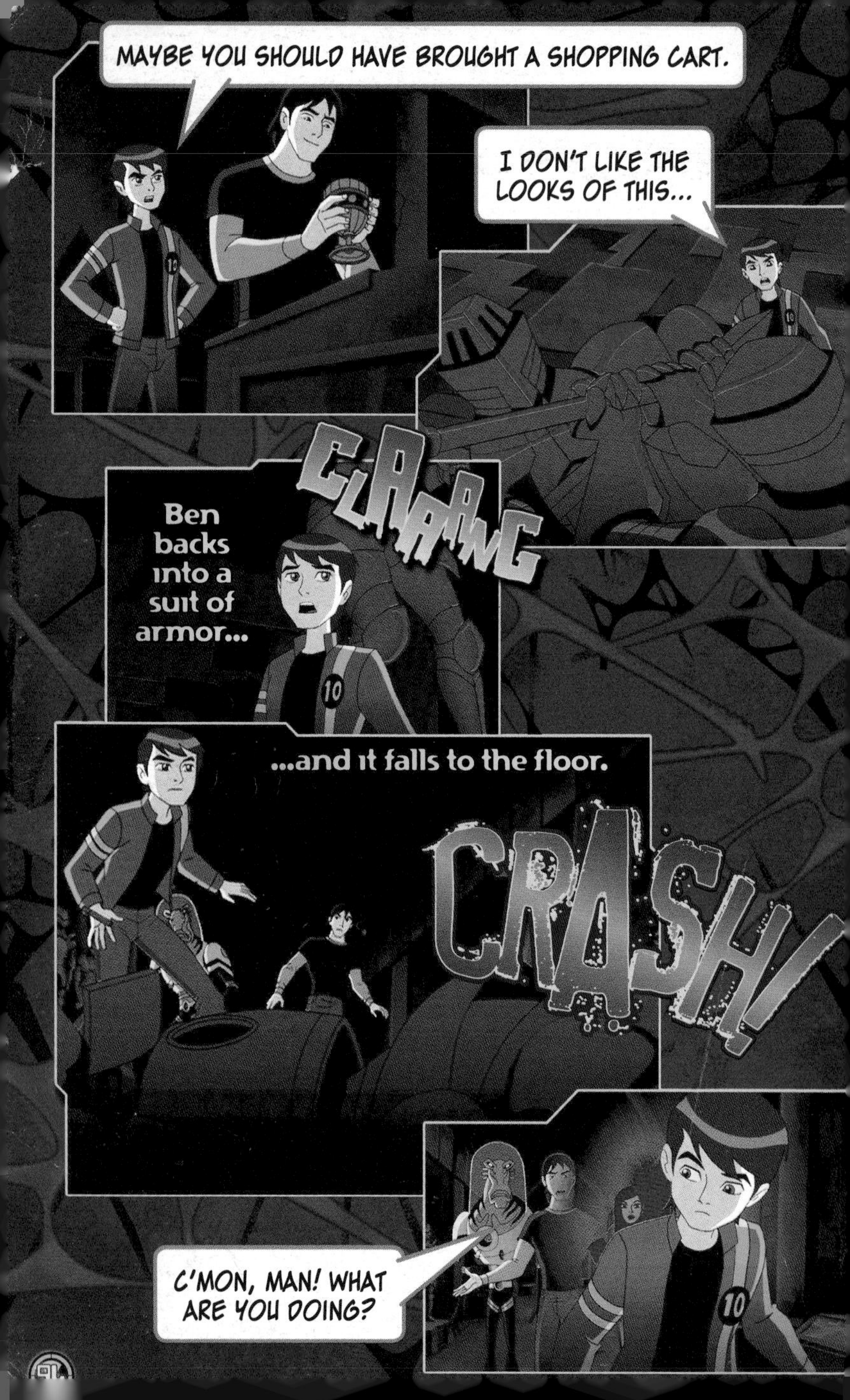
MAYBE YOU SHOULD HAVE BROUGHT A SHOPPING CART.
I DON'T LIKE THE LOOKS OF THIS...
CLAAANG
Ben backs into a suit of armor...
...and it falls to the floor.
CRASH!
C'MON, MAN! WHAT ARE YOU DOING?

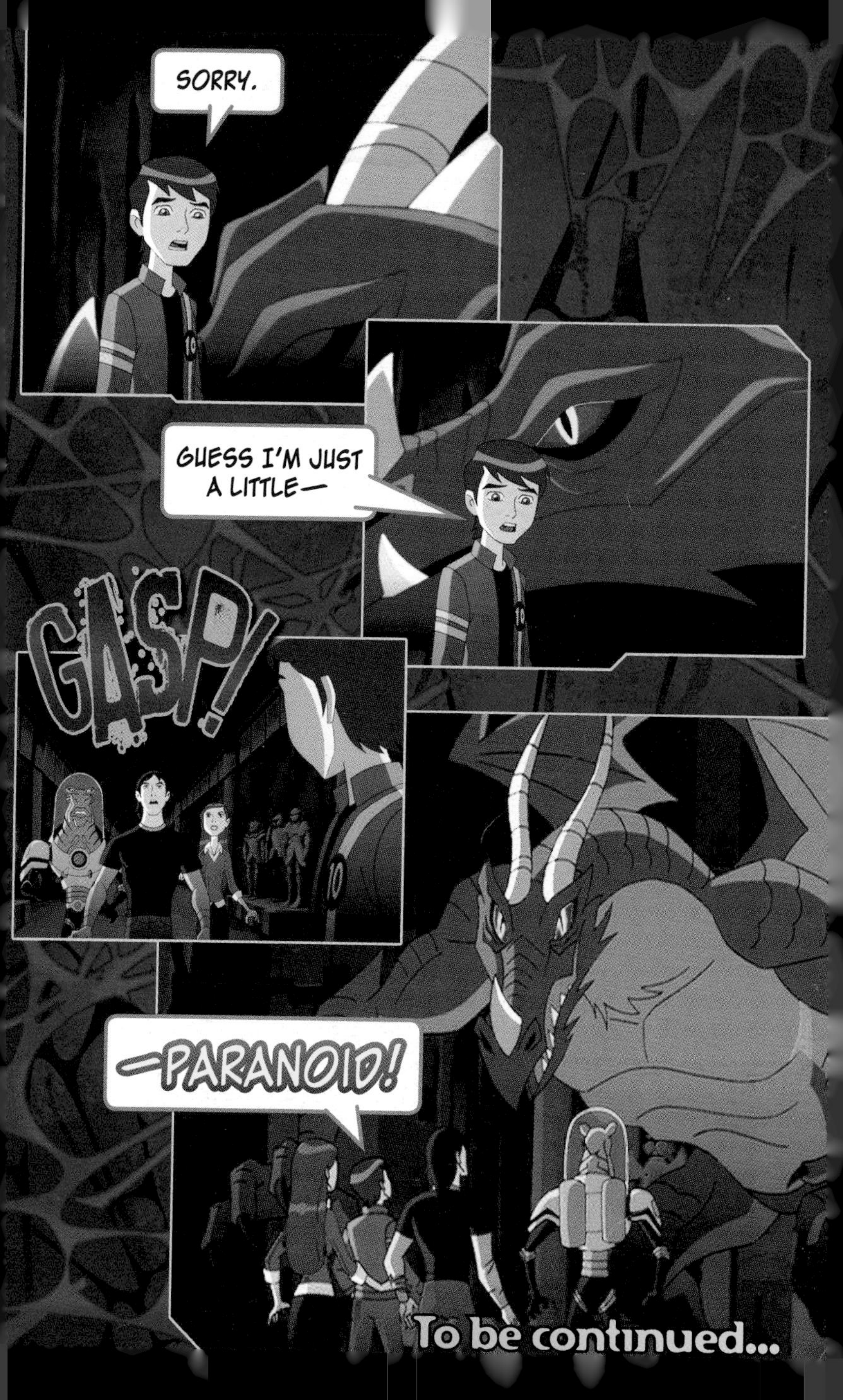

SORRY.
GUESS I'M JUST A LITTLE—
GASP!
—PARANOID!
To be continued...

PREVIEW OF BEN 10 ALIEN FORCE VOL. 2

AFTER DEFEATING THE FOREVER KNIGHTS, BEN, GWEN AND KEVIN FOLLOW A LEAD THAT TAKES THEM TO A SECRET BASE IN THE DESERT. THERE THEY HOPE TO LOCATE THEIR MISSING GRANDPA... BUT INSTEAD THEY FIND A SPACESHIP WITH A GIANT CANNON THE HIGHBREED INTEND TO USE TO DESTROY A NEARBY CITY. CAN THE TRIO STOP THE SHIP BEFORE IT'S TOO LATE?